Barry Arthur was born in London in 1950 and lived in England until, at the age of twenty-two, he boarded a ship to Australia. For the next thirty years he travelled extensively, living in France, Spain, England and Australia, and working intermittently, when unavoidable, as a Chartered Loss Adjuster. He currently lives with his wife, Linda, on a six-acre property in the Swan Valley, Western Australia.

Over the Wall to

Andalucía

Barry Arthur

Ashcroft Publishing

OVER THE WALL TO ANDALUCÍA

An Ashcroft Publishing book

Ashcroft Publishing
41 Dalgety Road, Middle Swan,
Western Australia, 6056

National Library of Australia
Cataloguing-in-Publication entry:

Arthur, Barry
Over the Wall to Andalucía / Barry Arthur

ISBN: 978-0-9870678-1-4

To Linda, who shared the adventure.

CHAPTER ONE

That spring I spent two months making bikinis on a hand-operated Singer sewing machine. I intended strolling the beaches of the French Riviera in the summer, selling them to attractive tourists. This venture was not meant to be a long-term career, you must understand, but merely a *divertissement* while I waited for fate to put in an appearance.

I was alone at my mother's cottage in an isolated part of Ardèche in the south of France. The climate is not as good as the French pretend it is and that April the mistral brought flurries of snow. The cottage was as primitive as the bikini production and the only heating was a blackened-stone fireplace. I soon discovered that there was a *problème sérieux* with the chimney. It worked well on calm days when I really did not need the fire, but with Gallic perverseness, if the mistral blew, clouds of smoke billowed into the room and gave me the choice of either choking or freezing to death. The house was built above an underground stream and, after heavy rain, water seeped up through the concrete floor and pooled in the dips. The disused goat shed was the bathroom. Its facilities were a water jug and bowl on a rickety card table, and a chemical toilet that always needed emptying. If I had not been a sole operator, I would have formed a union and gone on strike.

One morning in early May, fate arrived on cue in the shape of postman Pierre. He hated delivering mail to the house and I heard his bad-tempered tooting as he approached along the boggy track. I walked outside and Pierre greeted me sourly.

'*Une lettre d'Angleterre.*' He poked his head out of the window and morosely inspected the spattered side of his shiny yellow Citroen. '*Merde!*'

'Actually, Pierre, it's mud,' I pointed out, anticipating that he would appreciate some English humour.

He muttered something about *les Anglais* and let the letter fall to the ground. As I bent down, he gunned the engine and did his best to shower me with mud.

'*Merci,*' I called after the retreating Citroen. '*Au revoir.*'

The letter was from Linda. Two days later I packed a rucksack, locked up the house and my elderly Bedford Dormobile, and walked four miles to catch a bus to the station where I started the long train journey to Paris. This was years before the fast and super-smooth TGV, and the train rattled its way through rural France stopping at every hamlet and once at a place where there was no station, just a lone figure by the tracks, holding up his hand. I spent a cold and uncomfortable night at Gare de Lyon and in the morning I went across Paris on the metro and caught a bus to Calais. I crossed the channel to Dover and forty hours after leaving

Ardèche I reached Victoria Coach Station.

At 1 a.m. I was certain that Linda wasn't coming, but it was just her car; it had broken down three times en route from Bristol. Linda had the worst company car in the whole of England. It was an ancient, two-cylinder Fiat 500 that her boss had offered her as a joke when she had arrived late for work and complained about the buses. Linda had accepted, but the car proved to be no more reliable than the public transport she had abandoned. During its long life the Fiat suffered from every known automotive ailment and many that were mysteriously intermittent and never diagnosed. Just when you had cured one malady another would strike and lay it low. The RAC patrolmen around Bristol came to know the Fiat and when they spotted it wheezing along, with its faded blue paintwork, patchy white-wall tyres and flapping sunshine roof, they would hoot and call out, 'Still going then is it, my lovely?' They were a friendly and kind lot who did not seem to mind the constant calls to attend to the hypochondriac Fiat, but it helped that Linda was young and beautiful.

On the return journey, the Fiat stopped abruptly at 3.30 a.m. somewhere near Swindon. We didn't mind. We had almost a year to catch up on.

'Fuel vaporization,' said the yawning patrolman. 'Let the engine cool down and it should start.'

The car behaved after that, but by the time we reached Bristol it was light.

We were married in a hurry. Our parting in Australia twelve months before had been messy and traumatic, and our parents had made it clear that they were

9

strongly opposed to us reuniting. We believed that our only option was to present our marriage as a *fait accompli* and bear their wrath, knowing that, in time, they would forgive us. We paid extra for a special licence, which is reserved for people who elope, and took the place of a couple who had changed their mind.

On our wedding day, Linda left the flat punctually at seven-thirty in the morning to go to work. She was having second thoughts and I was not convinced she would return. She reached a decision at ten-thirty and went in to see her boss.

'I have to go out for a few hours and I need you to look after the office.'

'Why?'

'I'm getting married at eleven-thirty.'

He looked at his watch. 'Then you'd better hurry.'

I loitered at the flat and at five past eleven I had given up. I knew that, even if Linda had decided to go through with our wedding, there was a strong possibility that the capricious Fiat had let her down. Then I heard the sewing-machine engine. Linda had detoured to buy two white carnations.

The Fiat was heroic. Every light was green and we arrived with three minutes to spare. We pinned on the carnations, took our vows, and two secretaries witnessed us sign the register. Our wedding photographs are against the backdrop of the stone wall at the front of the registry office. I took a photograph of Linda and, afterwards, she photographed me. Something wasn't right and Linda pointed out that after people get married they are usually in the same photograph. There was no one around, so I balanced the camera on the sloping bonnet of the Fiat, set it to automatic, and dashed back to Linda. Just as we were about to leave, an elderly man walked by and Linda asked him if he would take our photograph. It was only then that we noticed his left arm was missing. The old-fashioned Minolta camera was fitted with a bulky lens, which made it heavy and awkward to use. We stood with our arms around each other and watched the man struggle. Eventually, he hunched his right shoulder, tilted his head to the left, pushed the camera to his eye and pressed the button. As a result, in the only two wedding photographs of us together, we are lurching either to the left or to the right, and in one to the left we look worried.

We had made no plans and for an hour we walked the streets, entwined, not talking, grinning like fools. Later, Linda dropped me at the flat and went back to work, where her boss presented her with a huge bouquet of flowers and a bundle of invoices to type. The unusual start to our married life set the pattern for the years that followed.

In July, we went to France for our honeymoon. We collected the Bedford van from my mother's cottage, loaded the bikinis and sewing machine, and drove to a camping ground near St Tropez, which we made our headquarters. The Bedford Dormobile had 1960's, state-of-the-art technology. The roof elevated, giving us eight feet of standing room. The front and rear seats folded flat and cunningly slid together to form the world's most uncomfortable double bed, with springs

11

and metal brackets that dug into us like arrow heads. There was a tiny plastic sink with pump-up water, and a two-ring gas stove. It was one step up from sleeping under canvas.

We walked for hours along the beaches, with rows of wispy bikinis made from exotic sari material dangling from our arms, but the women objected to being disturbed during the serious business of acquiring a suntan, and it was hot and unrewarding work. We discovered that the easiest place to sell the bikinis was on the campsite, where the holidaymakers were looking for a distraction. They gathered round the moment we set up the camping table and sewing machine, and with a wonderful lack of modesty German and Swedish girls ripped off their clothes to try on the bikinis. If we didn't have the right sizes, I would sit at the table in a state of euphoria and make them to order.

'This could be the start of our swimwear empire,' I said to Linda.

'I really don't think so,' she said. 'For a start, I'd feel a lot happier about this if it wasn't only women taking their clothes off.'

My family and friends had watched my bikini-making enterprise with cynical amusement. From his accountant's office in London, my brother, Neil, mimicked our grandmother whenever we spoke. 'It's about time you settled down and got yourself a proper job, Barry. Jesus, making bikinis!'

I tried to tell him about the Swedish and German girls. 'I don't want to hear about them,' he interrupted.

'In case you've forgotten, you're married.'

A year of freedom from working at a "proper" job and a taste of the simple, rural life in France had made me yearn for something different. I did not see that being married meant that I had to chain myself to a desk and a mortgage for the next forty years, and I had other plans. Nevertheless, within five weeks of returning from our honeymoon, I found myself again working as an insurance loss adjuster, complete with a company car and a mortgage on a semi-detached house in the suburbs of Bristol. Linda had relinquished the Fiat and was driving the Bedford van which, to my surprise, had accomplished the journey back from France and proved to be more reliable than the Fiat. Our parents had forgiven us and I was settling into my new job. Life was normal; that is, until one cold and drizzly weekend in November.

I opened the *Exchange and Mart* at the overseas property section. *Whitewashed cottages in Andalucía, set amongst olive and lemon groves and nestling in the foothills of the Sierra Nevada. Some with Mediterranean views.* What images that conjured up! I was straight away back at my mother's cottage, but the sun was shining and Linda was lounging around in one of my bikinis.

I looked outside at the grey. 'We must go and live in Andalucía.'

'Why must we?' asked Linda. 'We've only just moved in here and you've finally started a real job.'

Now Linda was starting to sound like my grandmother. 'Because France is cold and Spain is hot. It's exotic and it costs nothing to live there, and now

Franco's dead we won't be shot if we say the wrong thing. Because we're young and we have a lifetime to work at regular jobs and pay off mortgages, but most of all it will be an adventure.'

'Our parents have only just recovered from us getting married.'

'Well, we won't tell them yet.'

CHAPTER TWO

Six months after we were married, with Thatcherism on the horizon and poised to change Britain forever, we flew to Malaga, took the *Alsina* bus to Castell, and walked across the plaza into the bar of the *Hotel Brisa*. We had matching orange backpacks, well-polished hiking boots, and a lot of optimism.

Castell was a fishing village that tourists sped through on their way to Marbella and Torremolinos, and the round, grey-haired owner looked at us in surprise. Any tourists who came to Castell in winter were unusual, but the sort without a car were unheard of. There was no reason for them to be here, unless they were driving and became so tired that they had to stop. They would look at the drab plaza and hobble about on the stony beach for a few minutes; then realize that they were not as tired as they had originally thought and continue their journey.

In phrasebook Spanish, I asked for a room.

His face twisted in pain. '*Qué?*'

'*Un habitación.*'

He contorted his face further, before it cleared. '*Comprendo. Un habitación. Bueno.*'

We became used to the grimaces of the men in the hotel bar as they strained to understand us and, through the haze of tobacco smoke, we watched their faces work as they silently said words for us. They wanted to know why these *loco ingléses* had come to buy a *cortijo* in the area they were so desperate to leave. They spoke in a strange dialect, in loud, staccato bursts, and their hands slapped the wooden top of the bar when they talked. This was another language; not the Spanish of our phrasebooks.

We lacked the vocabulary to explain the purity of their lives compared to the materialistic world of ours. We tried to tell them that what they had was precious, but all they knew was the drudgery and the boredom as they scratched out an existence; and the awful poverty that for generations had repressed the people. Flat, fertile land was scarce and, elsewhere, the long, harsh summers made cultivation of anything but the hardiest plants impossible. The grape vines and the stunted almond and fig trees that dotted the hillsides struggled to survive, and produced a miserable return for the backbreaking toil of the *muleros* who ploughed the rocky slopes behind farting mules, and for the hunched peasants who picked the meagre fruit in the searing heat of summer.

But the land still produced more than the sea. The fishermen went out before dawn in their rowing boats and returned, hours later, with half a bucket of *sardinas* and *calamares*. The waiting wives kept what they needed and sold what was left at the market for a few pesetas. The men bought litres of thin, sharp wine that ate into their stomachs, and drank and slept the

16

days away on the beach in the shade of their boats.

But we were young and saw only the romance. We were pursuing an ideal and had yet to find out the reality.

We were waiting for Carlos Risueño, the estate agent whose advertisement had caught my eye six weeks before. When he arrived, we discovered that he had been to university in England and had an English wife. He spoke flawless English with a sexy accent, was good looking in a dark and mysterious way, and women fell in love with him. I was instantly and irrationally hostile. My career as a loss adjuster had made me short on trust in general, and in particular with an estate agent who was better looking than I and had mesmerized my wife. As a consequence, our negotiations with Carlos were unevenly balanced. I was bellicose and untrusting; whereas Carlos was reasonableness and charm, and Linda positioned herself midway between us.

Carlos had a list of rural properties for sale and the first hamlet he drove us to in his new Jeep was Los Morales. It is a cluster of whitewashed houses that tumble down a steep hillside five miles inland from Castell along the *rambla* - a wide and dusty river bed that slopes gently up from the Mediterranean. At the foot of the hillside is a bamboo-lined *barranco* - a small stream that trickles water all year round and produces a green oasis among the brown hills. On either side of the *barranco,* tiny, stone-walled fields were planted with rows of runner beans twisting up tripods made from bamboo canes. Citrus and custard-apple trees edged the fields, and almond trees covered the slopes. It was Yeats' bee-loud glade.

The property that was for sale was on the opposite side of the *barranco* from Los Morales - a whitewashed *cortijo* named Los Sanchez, which had an acre of flat, arable land. One side of the farmhouse was in a terrible state, with a section of the roof caved-in and lime plaster falling from the walls in slabs. There was no electricity or running water and the floors were either crumbling concrete or compacted mud - but to us it was perfect and we fell in love. We were reluctant to buy the first property we had looked at, and for two days we raced along narrow tracks, criss-crossed dry rivers, and corkscrewed up mountain paths to be shown abandoned *cortijos* that were described by Carlos as authentic Andalucían homes, unique character properties, and handyman's dreams, but most would have benefited from a bulldozer.

At the end of the second day, Carlos said, with his charming smile, that as we were such lovely and educated people, he and his wife, Carol, would like us to join them for a barbeque at a very special property that was for sale. The following day, they drove us miles into the mountains to an isolated *cortijo* with spectacular views over slopes and valleys to the Mediterranean. The property appeared to be the equivalent of a manor house, but it was far too remote for us to be interested. Carlos used the outdoor fireplace to cook the fish that he had bought from the market that morning. Carol collected herbs from the hillside and picked lemons and oranges from the orchard. The day was idyllic - sunny and mild, with a gentle breeze drifting across the slopes - and we were being shown what life would be like living in Andalucía - every day magical, just like today.

Carol was a rare type of woman who oozed sexuality. It seeped from her pores and cast a spell over any male within twenty yards. Sitting at the table on the terrace, warmed by the sun and a considerable amount of wine, I found that my eyes were being drawn, with increasing frequency, to her scoop-necked blouse that, strangely, appeared to be getting lower as the afternoon progressed. Linda saw me looking and refused to speak to me on the drive back, but later that evening, when we were again talking, we agreed that Carol and Carlos made a formidable sales team.

The next day we rang Carlos and told him we had decided to buy Los Sanchez and we would like to visit the property again before we signed the contract. Carlos drove us there that afternoon. When we arrived, there was a man in the field, weeding around the base of an orange tree with a mattock. He stopped what he was doing, walked over and introduced himself as José Manzano. He was short, wiry, with a creased face and a three-day growth of beard. He was wearing a flat cap and had a half-smoked cigarette hanging from the corner of his mouth. When we got to know José better, we discovered that the cigarette was a fixture and his three-day growth did not vary for weeks on end. It defied science by remaining at this length. Every now and then he would shave it off, but the next day it would return as a three-day growth. We never discovered the reason for this phenomenon and put it down to a genetic oddity. José and Carlos spoke together at machine-gun speed for a few minutes and it was clear that they were discussing Los Sanchez.

'José,' explained Carlos, when they had finished, 'is a poor *campesino,* who was a good friend of the previous owner, Antonio Sanchez. After he died, the family moved away and they told José that he could use the land to grow vegetables. He has spent money fertilising the soil and he wants to know if you will permit him to carry on using the *campo* until you need it.'

José appeared to be expecting the worst and he watched us with a scowl while he kicked the blade of his mattock. We told Carlos that we would be happy if José continued to work the land and look after the trees until we came to live at the *cortijo*. When Carlos translated our reply, José's face cracked into a smile, revealing four brown teeth that didn't connect. We later found out that he ate with a circular movement of his lower jaw, mashing rather than chewing his food - like a blender on slow. He rattled off a stream of words out of the left side of his mouth, while the cigarette remained glued to the right side, jerking about. When he showed no sign of stopping, Carlos interrupted him.

'He says that, as the owners of the land, you are entitled to half of everything that he grows. It is *costumbre.*'

Whether or not it was the custom, I couldn't see us coming over to Spain to collect a few kilos of vegetables and, besides, it seemed an unfair apportionment when José was doing all the work. I looked at Linda and she shook her head.

'No,' I said, 'we don't want anything. All we would

like José to do is keep an eye on the *cortijo* for us.'

After Carlos translated, José beamed and stuck out his hand. A lifetime of wielding a mattock had grown calluses on top of calluses and it was like gripping the shell of a tortoise. There was something completely transparent and honest about José and Linda and I beamed back at him.

Carlos drove us to his office - which turned out to be the foyer of the local bank - and we signed the contract. Afterwards, he told us that Los Sanchez was his first sale and we were the only foreigners to own property in the area.

The day before we flew back to England, we walked the uneven, rock-strewn track up the *rambla* from Castell to Los Sanchez, our feet puffing up the grey, river-bed dust, which coated our boots and legs. We passed faded clumps of gorse and broom, occasional stands of oleander, and swathes of lemon thyme that perfumed the air as we brushed against it. We came to whitewashed *cortijos* and hamlets where the families hung over their balconies to watch our approach. We smiled and waved until, finally, they smiled in return and called out *adios* and *vaya con Dios* as they made pushing movements with their hands to speed our journey. One very old woman gave the sign of the cross and shuffled inside.

After nearly two hours, we arrived at Los Sanchez. The house was locked. We had no key and we sat on the stone wall alongside the front door. We ate crusty bread with sardines from a can while, one hundred yards away at Los Morales, a fat woman dressed in black propped her elbows on the rail of her balcony and studied us. Her husband, greyhound-thin, stood next to her, and a boy and a girl, half-hidden, looked round them. We waved, but they didn't respond.

We had not brought the heavy Minolta camera to Spain, and Linda sat and sketched Los Sanchez while I explored the stone outhouses and our neighbours continued to watch us. When we left I waved and, this time, the man and the woman waved back.

CHAPTER THREE

We estimated that it would take us nearly two years to repay our loan for Los Sanchez and then we would sell our home in Bristol and move to Spain. We were going to live there forever and, like the locals, grow our own vegetables and keep rabbits and chickens. We would be self-sufficient and we would need money just for tiresome things like petrol. The problem was that our knowledge of plant cultivation and animal husbandry was limited to a few episodes of the *Good Life* and instructions on the backs of seed packets.

The months after we returned from Spain were frantic. We planned and we researched. We read everything there was to read about self-sufficiency, from crop rotation to cross-pollination, from beekeeping to tanning rabbit skins. We became theoretical experts and all that we needed now was the practice. We studied Spanish at evening classes, conjugated verbs over breakfast, and lisped all our Cs. We toured second-hand shops for old furniture that was in keeping with our *cortijo* and stripped it down to bare wood. The house reeked of teak oil and beeswax, and eventually became so congested that it was impossible to cross a floor without climbing over a piece of furniture destined for Andalucía. Doors never opened fully, forcing us to shuffle sideways into rooms, and the house resembled a badly-organised furniture depository.

It kept us busy through those winter months while we waited for the warmer weather - when we could dig up the useless flowerbeds and lawns and make our garden productive. When we did, we discovered that there was pottery-grade clay under the grass in the back garden and, after it rained, the ground became a quagmire. If we stood still for more than a few seconds it seized hold of our gumboots and refused to release them. There was no alternative but to leave the boots standing in the mud like sentries, and to mince, in our socks, over to the safety of the path, and then lay a plank over the bog to retrieve them. Every weekend we laboured to transform the garden - breaking up clods of clay, sieving and raking the soil, and planting rows of delicate seedlings. A few miles away at Filton, British Aircraft Corporation manufactured the Concorde and the planes regularly flew overhead, barely clearing our roof. We would stop work, lean on our forks and stare up, as the test pilots looked down the supercilious noses of their supersonic planes at our rustic toil.

I built a portable chicken house from plans in a self-sufficiency book. It was supposed to be easily carried by two people, but when it was completed it needed the help of four burly neighbours to drag it a few yards. The next Saturday morning we drove to a chicken farm in a nearby village, which advertised a variety of breeds for sale.

'If it's just for eggs, you're better off with hybrids,' said the man. 'Shaver 585s is what you need ... skinny things that don't eat a lot. Egg-laying machines, that's what they are. Hold the world record ... and they've got a good temperament ... make nice pets.'

He took us to a large shed that was built on poles and had enough room underneath for a man to stand upright. Inside were hundreds of identical brown chickens running around on a wire-mesh floor.

'Makes it dead easy to clean,' he said. 'The droppings just fall through.'

I pictured a stoic employee, wearing a wide-brimmed hat, coming along every few days to shovel up a mountain of manure. What wonderful creatures chickens are - to supply eggs, meat, feathers and fertiliser. I felt that we were already halfway to being self-sufficient.

We brought four hens home in a large cardboard box and opened it on the remaining section of back lawn. We had thought that, after spending their entire lives in a wire-floored shed, they would tear around the garden turning cartwheels, but they were surprisingly reluctant to leave the box. They craned their necks and peered over the sides, decided that they did not like what they saw and settled into a huddle.

We grasped the box and slowly turned it over while the hens squawked and beat their wings against the inside before, finally, all four were on the lawn. In the excitement, one of them laid an egg that, amazingly, remained unbroken on the grass. We walked away a few paces and the birds straightaway flew onto the upturned box and perched there, heads revolving in unison, alternately regarding us and the alien green substance with equal suspicion.

'They'll get used to it eventually,' I said. 'Let's leave them to it and we'll have our first egg for lunch.'

Linda laughed. 'Great! A one-egg omelette for two. We're not going to get fat on self-sufficiency.'

Afterwards, we found that the hens had left their sanctuary and were eating our lettuce seedlings. It took them several weeks to learn how to scratch for food and, after that, nothing in the garden was safe and they were confined to the run.

Our next door neighbour, Matt Ashford, was a strong, barrel-chested and recently retired Bristolian. He spoke with a deep west-country burr that conjured up images of milking sheds and hay-ricks and, after you finished talking to him, made you check the soles of your shoes. He had a large and impressive vegetable garden that was covered with mushroom compost and produced prolific quantities of Brussels sprouts, cabbages and potatoes. He grew serious crops and did not mess around with new-fangled vegetables, like snow peas. He was an expert and we were rank amateurs.

I first met Matt when he spoke to me over the side fence. 'Do you like beer?' he said, without preamble. He had spotted me from his lounge window and decided it was time we became acquainted.

It was not yet nine-thirty in the morning and I wasn't sure where the question was leading - whether it was simply the prelude to a discussion on the merits of beer compared to scrumpy, or if there was more to it, and I hesitated before nodding. He disappeared inside and returned a few minutes later with two full pint-mugs. He told me that he made the beer from a kit and promptly downed his in a couple of mouthfuls. I sipped it cautiously but it was delicious, full-flavoured and wonderfully smooth.

'That is one of the best beers I've ever tasted,' I told him.

'Arrh, it's Moorish,' said Matt and went inside to refill his glass.

Later that afternoon he passed me a bag of new potatoes over the fence. 'You'll love they,' he said, 'they're Moorish.'

I hadn't been aware that Morocco was famous for its beer and potatoes and thought it was more likely to be Belgium.

'Are you sure?' I asked.

'Arrh,' he said. 'You'll find out.'

I went inside to show Linda the potatoes and told her what Matt had said about them and his beer.

'You fool,' she said, 'he's saying they're *more-ish.*'

I had enormous difficulty with the west-country accent during the early days we lived in Bristol. As well as omitting the middle of words, Bristolians have the charming habit of putting the letter "L" onto the end of words that finish in a vowel, and people would go to the *operal* or visit *Americal.* Our television provided us with an entirely different language problem. Unaccountably, we received BBC Wales and, although many of the programmes were the same as the English BBC, occasionally some were broadcast in Welsh. I looked upon this as a quaint idiosyncrasy until the time of the Five Nations' rugby tournament. I turned on the television expecting to watch England playing at Twickenham. Instead, the broadcast was of Wales against Scotland. Here I was, an Englishman living in England and I was forced to watch two foreign teams. It was intolerable. I stormed into the back garden, spotted Matt Ashford, and started to rant.

'It be the *areal*,' he said.

'It can't be,' I said. 'We bought a new aerial when we moved in.'

He looked at me suspiciously. 'No, it be the *areal* where we live - next to Wales.'

I had similar problems at the scaffolding company where Linda worked. Immediately after we were married, she had persuaded her boss to give me a temporary position as a bottom hand, until I found a permanent job as a loss adjuster. I had a terrible three weeks trying to understand the scaffolders and they believed that Linda had married a simpleton. I would stand at the bottom of the scaffolding and, from a height of about twenty-five feet, they would call out what equipment they needed. I was all right with the poles, either *long uns* or *short uns*, but when it came to the various couplings I was completely lost. After they had repeated the request several times, I would take a wild guess and inevitably throw up the wrong ones. They would shout down unintelligible insults and issue fresh instructions, like commandments from the mount, and I would apologise and try again.

The long poles were heavy and difficult to handle, and there was a technique to keeping them balanced. My right hand had to be as high up the pole as I could reach and my left hand as far down. I would then struggle to lift the pole up to a scaffolder, who would reach down and take it from me, one-handed, as if it were a toothpick. One day I had been passing up *long uns* for what seemed like hours and my arms were rubbery. On about the fiftieth pole I could lift it so far, but no further. I tried with all my strength to raise it the extra two feet, but I was frozen in position, like a pole-vaulter at the start of his run. I heaved and grunted while the scaffolders grinned, but it was as though the pole was anchored. In desperation, I made the mistake of altering my grip. The balance of the pole changed and I began the irreversible process of overbalancing backwards. If I had let go of the pole it would have fallen on top of me, so I hung on with both hands and crashed over on to my back. The end of the pole struck the ground twenty feet behind me and narrowly missed the roof of a parked car. The men laughed so hard that one almost fell off the scaffolding.

They were a great bunch and treated me well, although that might have been something to do with the fact that Linda made up their wage packets. Once, after a typical day of misunderstandings, I was in Linda's office when one of the scaffolders stuck his head round the door.

'We be going *furtin* on Sunday. You *cummen*?'

I wasn't sure what *furtin* entailed, but I didn't like the sound of it. Linda had been working there for six months and when she was around she translated for me. I glanced at her and she gave an almost imperceptible shake of the head.

'Sorry,' I said, 'we're going to be busy this Sunday,

but thanks for asking.'

'I felt pretty sure,' said Linda, as we walked to the car, 'that you wouldn't want to go ferreting,'

For several months after I left the company and went to work as a loss adjuster, brawny scaffolders with tattoos and stubble came into Linda's office and asked after me. 'Is he all right, my lovely?' they'd enquire solicitously. 'Is he getting on better, now?'

Our next venture was rabbits. Matt Ashford donated an old sideboard and it was a simple matter to convert it to a hutch by replacing the floor with wire mesh and the centre panel of each door with chicken wire. On the way home from work, I called in to our local pet shop.

'You want two rabbits?' he repeated. 'Any particular type? I've got plenty of crosses or, if you want pure breeds, some Flemish Giants and Belgian Dwarfs.'

They sounded like characters out of Grimm's fairy tales. 'No, I don't mind, just so long as it's a male and a female.'

'Ah, then you must really want rabbits,' he said.

I chose two rabbits that were a cross between New Zealand Trolls and Greek Goblins, or something similar. They were large, white and had friendly expressions, but unfortunate red eyes, which I thought made them look shifty. I brought them home and Linda immediately named them Winnie and Ralph, after a couple of our friends they resembled. At that stage, it had not really sunk in that these rabbits or their offspring would end up on our dinner table.

As soon as I put them in the hutch, Ralph had only one thing on his mind and lumpily pursued Winnie round and round. I am convinced that he eventually wore her out and she acceded to his advances, not out of any enthusiasm, but from sheer exhaustion. Ralph seemed to be enjoying himself, but I am not so sure about her. I suspect that, if she'd been a woman, she would have been reading a magazine. As it was, during the whole episode, she chewed reflectively on a piece of dry grass and looked pensive. After a burst of frenetic activity, Ralph suddenly bit Winnie on the neck, went rigid, and toppled sideways from her back. She glanced around, saw that he'd finished, and hopped away, looking positively frisky. Ralph continued to lay there with his feet and nose quivering. My God, he's had a seizure! I rushed inside to fetch Linda.

Linda looked at Ralph's twitching body. She had read the section on mating that I'd skipped over. 'That's quite normal,' she pronounced. 'After intercourse, the buck collapses like that and it takes him a while to recover. I'd have thought you would have recognised the symptoms.'

At weekends, we let Winnie and Ralph out of the hutch to explore the garden. Like the hens, they were initially wary of everything, but they soon developed a taste for freedom and became harder and harder to catch. As we crept up on them, they would sense our intent and hurtle off, with us in pursuit. It was great fun, but one day they discovered the peas and, within the space of thirty seconds, they went along the row and nipped through each stem at ground level. It was the last time we let them out.

By the end of our first summer in Bristol we had run

out of room in the back garden and we were planting carrots and parsnips in the front flowerbeds. Our four hens were laying an egg a day each, which was more than we could eat, and Matt Ashford passed his metal bucket over neighbours' fences to be filled with kitchen peelings for the rabbits and chickens, in exchange for some of our excess eggs. Our efforts to learn Spanish were starting to pay off. We could count up to one hundred, ask someone the time; we knew the days of the week and months of the year; and we could tell any Spaniards who hadn't figured it out already that we were foreigners.

We were also harvesting a few vegetables, but we had found out that growing enough to eat, all year round, was impossible. There were too many things that conspired against us - birds, slugs and snails; mites, moulds and funguses; root rot, borers and wire-worms; aphids and caterpillars; lack of nutrient and so on - and that was disregarding the occasional escape of chickens and rabbits. It was dispiriting, after all the hard work, to bring into the kitchen a handful of maggoty peas. But we were learning a lot and we told ourselves that it would be much easier in the hot Spanish climate.

It didn't take us long to discover that rabbits breed like, well ... rabbits, and we spent several hours each weekend gathering edible weeds from the hedgerows to supplement the bought grain and kitchen scraps. We knew that soon we would have to carry out our plan to eat them, otherwise we would be overrun. In addition to Winnie and Ralph, we had six young rabbits of eating size and a two-week old litter of eight. We had housed the young rabbits in a separate hutch and Ralph was now in a cage on his own. He would sit for most of the day looking grumpy while he watched Winnie.

I had been putting off the day when I had to kill one of the young rabbits and I realised that there was a big difference between talking about breeding rabbits for the table and actually going to the cage and butchering one. Following our meagre rewards from the vegetable garden, for the first time I was having doubts about our intended lifestyle in Spain. I spoke about it to Linda.

'Look,' she said, 'how many times have you lectured our friends about the wholesome struggle of producing our own food, and told them that if they eat meat then they should be prepared to kill the animal - rather than let someone else do the dirty work and then buy it from the supermarket, sanitised and wrapped in plastic?'

'You're right, but why is it my job? Why don't you do it?

'Because men do the hunting; it's traditional. Besides, men are good at killing. That's why there aren't many women soldiers. Anyway, if you feel you can't do it, let's take them back to the pet shop.'

Goaded, I went outside, reached into the cage and grabbed the nearest rabbit. I went straight into the shed before I changed my mind, and killed it. It was ghastly. I couldn't look at Winnie and Ralph as I carried the dead rabbit past their cages. In the kitchen, I found that I was trembling so much I needed two glasses of dandelion wine before my hands were steady enough to skin and clean it. When I'd finished, I went into the lounge.

'You look pale,' said Linda. 'Are you all right?'

'I've just butchered one of the young rabbits. It was horrible. I'm thinking of becoming a vegetarian.'

I didn't, but the rabbit sat in our refrigerator for five days before I was able to eat it.

We became self-sufficiency fanatics and bought a marvellous book entitled *Farmhouse Fare*. It was full of old-fashioned recipes for things as diverse as pig curing; cheese making; cleaning agents made from ingredients like turpentine, vinegar and caustic soda; and there was a particularly unusual one for a blue fabric "reviver" that involved boiling up ivy leaves. We filled every shelf of the airing cupboard with bubbling demijohns of country wine and, as a result, we had a winter of musty sheets that were relegated to sharing the dank box-room alongside eggs preserved in buckets of isinglass, jars of homemade jam, and trays of last season's apples wrapped in newspaper. On rainy Sunday afternoons I would disappear upstairs to the airing cupboard to blend and sample concoctions of dandelion, parsnip and elderflower wine, and come downstairs a few hours later considerably worse for wear. Our friends became resigned to our obsessive behaviour and made polite remarks about cloudy and still fermenting wines while they bravely ate beetroot-leaf and turnip-top salad. One weekend, things came to a head when my brother, Neil, and his wife, Lesley, came to stay.

Neil emerged from the bathroom. 'What's that disgusting mess in the washbasin?'

'I don't know,' I said, thinking it must be something to do cheese-making, probably curdled milk draining through a pair of Linda's tights. 'What does it look like?'

'A sticky blob of congealed porridge and it smells foul.'

I realised what he was talking about. 'That's homemade oatmeal soap. It's all natural ingredients.'

'I don't care what it is; I'm not washing with it. I'm going out to buy some Palmolive. What is wrong with you? Life's hard enough as it is without going back to the dark ages to make it twice as difficult. The whole point of inventing things like bars of soap is so you don't spend hours boiling up string and bacon rind, or whatever that mess is, in order to save a few pence. It's bad enough that you two have gone completely batty, but when you start inflicting it on other people ...'

After that, we stopped experimenting on our family and friends, and our failures, such as whey cheese and stinging-nettle soup, were fed discreetly to the chickens.

CHAPTER FOUR

Within eighteen months we had paid off the loan for Los Sanchez and we could at last finalise our preparations for moving to Andalucía. We had collected together a huge assortment of furniture and equipment that we would need in Spain and would be difficult or expensive to obtain there. We had bought everything second hand and at little cost - including a smoke-blackened Calor-gas cooker out of a fire-damaged caravan, a 350-gallon black-plastic drum that had been used to export orange juice from Israel; and a 250-gallon corrugated-iron tank, in which a farmer from Somerset had stored diesel. The two containers were for our water supply and I spent a claustrophobic afternoon inside them with a scrubbing brush and detergent. Once, I arrived home from work and found a pile of planks and timber posts on the front lawn, liberated from a building site somewhere and dropped off by a helpful scaffolding lorry. A friend who was renovating her kitchen gave us her old sink unit, and we swapped a few dozen eggs and some garden vegetables for a chipped enamel bath. Someone locally advertised two chemical toilets for sale and we bought them both. We visited every second-hand book shop in Bristol and bought classic children's books by authors like Enid Blyton and Richmal Crompton. We were planning a long way ahead.

We drew up an inventory of the items and made an appointment to visit the Spanish Consulate in Southampton. We took with us every document that we thought they could possibly ask for - from birth certificates and bank statements down to old electricity bills and library tickets. We emerged, drained, several hours later, reeling from the information that we would have to pay import duty on our possessions. The official told us, however, that we would be able to recover the duty if we could prove in two years' time that the items had not been imported for commercial purposes. He was unable to offer any practical suggestions on how we could accomplish this, except to say that it might be possible to obtain a notarised declaration by someone of high-standing in the community, such as the local priest, to the effect that our possessions after two years were the same ones we had arrived with. I felt that the likelihood of finding a friendly priest who was prepared to come to the *cortijo* immediately after we arrived and tick off all the items on the inventory, and then come back two years later and repeat the process, was extremely remote and I mentally waved goodbye to the import duty. This was our first experience of Spanish bureaucracy and a foretaste of the tangled mass of regulations we would later encounter in Spain - which we were to discover make all other trials of life appear minor. The unforeseen cost of the import duty, added to the expense of hiring a removal van and the price of the ferry to Spain, made us now wonder if it was really worthwhile taking the stuff over there. But we had spent 18 months collecting it all and we knew that to buy everything in that part of Spain - either new, or in the rare second hand shops that sold "antiques" and collectibles to the tourists at insane prices - would cost us twice as much. So, we paid the import duty to the Spanish Consulate.

In June we took two week's holiday from our jobs and hired a 3½-ton removal truck to transport our possessions to Los Sanchez. This was the largest vehicle we could drive on our group-A licences and it seemed enormous. I asked Linda to help me reverse out of the yard and she stood in the only spot at the back of the truck where I couldn't see her in either wing mirror. A grinning employee watched me nearly demolish the boundary fence and I could see us spending the £200 excess several times over before we had even left the yard. Out on the road the truck turned out to be straightforward to drive, everything pretty much the same as a car - just a lot bigger. I discovered that turning left was the only delicate manoeuvre, which required leaving a much greater distance between the vehicle and the kerb. On my first attempt at a left turn, two pedestrians leapt for safety and shook their fists as the truck mounted the pavement. After that, I managed to keep it on the road.

We had all day Saturday to load the truck before catching the ferry from Plymouth to Santander early on Sunday morning. By 2 o'clock on Saturday afternoon the truck was full, although more than half our furniture was still on the pavement. We were sitting on the kerb in despair, praying for a miracle or a quick death, when my tennis partner, Andy Crocombe, and his girlfriend, Vicky, drove up. They had come, unasked, to see if we needed any help. Andy glanced at our expressions and went over to the truck and studied the inside. 'That, Arthur,' he said, 'is the worst job of packing I have ever seen.'

They helped us remove everything from the truck. Andy cast an educated eye over the items littering the pavement and our front garden, before he directed operations with meticulous strategic planning, like a youthful Rommel. He ordered us to take out all the clothes, bedding, kitchen equipment and small items that we had packed into tea chests and cardboard boxes, and instead put the items inside the two water containers, and then to fill every wardrobe, cupboard and drawer. He judged the best order to put each large item in and then crammed every inch of space around it with smaller items before he allowed us to bring in another piece. With Andy's skill and unfailing good humour, we re-packed the truck in less than two hours and, this time, only a handful of things remained on the footpath, including a faithful, musty old duffel bag that contained my Luton Grammar School sports kit, which Linda had steadfastly refused to pack on health grounds. When she wasn't looking, I squeezed it in behind a stack of chairs.

'You owe us a meal, Arthur,' said Andy and offered me some advice before they zoomed off to save someone else's life. 'When you get there, take the things out the same way we packed them in, except do it the other way round. Do you think you'll be able to

39

remember that?'

When we arrived at Plymouth docks the following morning, the ferry official said that we were using the vehicle for commercial purposes and the rate was twice that of a private vehicle. We would have to pay the extra cost; otherwise he would not let us on.

'This is not a commercial trip,' I said. 'We are transporting *our* possessions from *our* house in England to *our* house in Spain. Where is the commerce in that?' I showed him the importation documents from the Spanish Consulate.

'It doesn't make any difference,' the official said. 'It's a commercial vehicle.'

'We've paid for the length and height of this vehicle, so it makes no difference if it's a car and a caravan or this truck; it still takes up exactly the same amount of room. Anyway, no one said anything when we booked it.'

Something happens to certain people when you put them in uniform, especially if it has a shirt with brightly coloured epaulettes. In a different life this man would have carried a swagger cane and screamed orders on a parade ground. The use of logic inflamed him. His attitude had now hardened and it didn't matter what I said, he was not going to budge. Linda tried pleading with him and brought a slight concession. If there was any room left on the boat, after they had loaded all the other vehicles, he would let us on. We seethed for an hour as we watched the lines of vehicles drive past us on to the ferry and we prayed that it wouldn't be full. Just when they were about to raise the back of the boat, and we were resigned to the fact that we wouldn't get on, he casually gestured us through.

Our drive from Santander to Los Sanchez covered the length of Spain - from Cantabria on the Bay of Biscay, to the province of Granada on the Mediterranean. The route took us over five mountain ranges and across the endless, central high plain that surrounds Madrid. The roads were, without exception, dreadful. I drove for hours until, late at night, I became too tired and Linda took over while I dozed. It was the first time she had driven the truck, but there were no mountains for several hours and the traffic was light. Half-an-hour later, I was groggily awake and thought for a moment we were back on the boat. We were snaking along a completely empty, straight stretch of road. As Linda drifted over to the wrong side of the road, she over-corrected and went almost onto the gravel edge. She again swung the wheel and the same thing occurred on the other side. The oscillations were becoming greater and it seemed that the only way they would stop was when we ended up in a ditch. I grabbed hold of the wheel and together we eased the truck to the correct side of the road and stopped. The problem was that Linda hadn't slept either and was as tired as I was. We went to sleep in the cab for a few hours and, afterwards, I carried on driving. Two and a half days after we left Santander, and less than fifty miles from Los Sanchez, we were flagged down by two policemen who were standing on either side of the road. The one on the far side stayed where he was and the other one asked for our papers.

He studied the documents. 'Your licence is for a car and a motorcycle only. It does not permit you to drive this *camión*.'

'It does in England.'

'But you are not in England and you cannot drive it any further.'

I groaned. Getting this stuff to Los Sanchez had become like the labours of Hercules. 'We're nearly there,' I said to Linda. 'We'll just have to pay someone to drive us this last bit and take a chance getting back home.'

'Where are you going?' said the policeman.

'We have bought a *cortijo* inland from Castell de Ferro and we are moving permanently to Spain.'

'I myself am from that region. What is the name of your *cortijo*?'

'Los Sanchez - next to Los Morales.'

'That is *increíble!* I am from Los Carlos, three kilometres away. So, you have bought Antonio Sanchez's old house. I know his son; he too is a policeman.'

We were now old friends - family almost. The matter of the licence was trivial, a technicality. We had driven this far; it proved we were safe on the roads. 'But it is possible that other policemen you may encounter will be more *riguroso*, so I shall tell you the way to get to Los Sanchez avoiding the main roads.' He gave us directions from our map, which involved driving high into the Alpujarras on what appeared to be goat tracks, and then fording rivers and abseiling down the sides of mountains.

'Will the *camión* be all right on these roads?' Linda

asked.

'Of course, *senora*, the large *butano camiónes* use them all the time.'

With handshakes and best wishes for our new life he waved us on our way. In between changing from first to fourth gear, we debated whether to take the back way and decided we would rather risk another run in with the police than toppling over the edge of a mountain. We stayed on the main roads and arrived at Los Sanchez, without incident, two hours later.

The *cortijo* had deteriorated little in eighteen months. More render had fallen from the external walls and the exposed mud had streaked the whitewash below; another section of the roof had caved in, but not much else had changed. José Manzano had planted a third of the field with potatoes and the remainder with *habichuelas* - Spanish runner beans - a head-high jungle covering the tripods of canes. The afternoon we arrived, José walked up the *rambla* from his home in the next hamlet, La Venta. He emerged soundlessly on the terrace and announced himself with a low, hoarse cough, like an asthmatic sheep. Had we come to live? Was the *camión* ours? In which case, did we want to take some sacks of *habichuelas* back with us? We were anxious to unload the essential items and at least have a bed to sleep in that night, so we thanked José and told him we would talk to him later. But he was in no hurry to leave and he sat on the wall alongside the front door, smiling and nodding at us. He offered me a cigarette and lit one for himself, before he let fly with an extraordinary outpouring. We spent the next half hour listening to him and watching him make sweeping gestures that encompassed most of the surrounding hillsides - the whole time not having the slightest idea what he was talking about. We finally decided that etiquette had been satisfied and escorted him down the front path, with friendly pats on the shoulder, as he continued to talk and wave his arms around.

We had only seven days at Los Sanchez before we had to leave for England to return the truck and go back to work. It took us two full days to unload the vehicle and carry, drag or push everything up the steep path from the *barranco* to the house. We had a lot of accidents. Much of our furniture received fresh scratches and chips, and as we were heaving the 250-gallon corrugated-iron tank up the path it twisted sideways near the top and rolled over the edge, dropping fifteen feet into the field below. It demolished a few of José's runner beans, but, miraculously, the tank survived with only a few dents. We camped in two rooms and stored our possessions throughout the house in other rooms where the roof was reasonably intact. We lived most of the time outside and cooked on a small open fire on the terrace, where we set up our dining-room table and chairs.

The shortness of our visit heightened our senses and we drank everything in. The coolness of the early mornings and the pockets of still, moist air in the *barranco*; the smell of broom and gorse blending with the wood smoke from our fire; the swallows diving and turning all around us; the constant low drone of the insects and the lazy voices of the *campesinos* calling to each other in the fields, with occasional words we could

44

understand.

By midday it had changed; the temperature had risen and the sun burned our skin; the air was drier and dustier; the *campesinos* were leaving the fields to go home; the swallows were now dots wheeling overhead and the cicadas had come awake, drowning out the other sounds. Little moved in the afternoon. It was the time the sun ruled. The light was no longer sharp and a haze had formed around the hills. It was difficult to separate colours that a few hours before had been vivid. People and animals slept.

The evenings were like silk, as the warmth of the day gradually seeped away. Later, soft cool currents invaded from the mountains and, on the terrace, we wrapped ourselves in a blanket and looked up at the biggest, blackest sky in the world.

On the third day, we drove into Castell for a swim and to buy provisions. Fully laden, the truck had sat solidly and had ridden easily over the bumps and potholes in the *rambla*, but unladen it was an entirely different vehicle. At anything above ten miles per hour it bucked and reared, threw us out of our seats and burst open the back doors. It took us half an hour to travel the five miles and we arrived shattered. The inside of the truck was coated with grey dust.

'Right,' I said, 'we've now established that this is not the ideal vehicle for the terrain. I just hope the Bedford copes better than this; otherwise our excursions from Los Sanchez will be rare events.'

When we came back from Castell, we walked over to Los Morales on the opposite side of the *barranco* to meet our neighbours, Fra'quito and Adela, who had stood and watched us from their balcony 18 months before. I explained that we had come to deliver our furniture and were staying for only a week, but we would be returning to live permanently once we had sold our house in England. When they didn't say anything, I wasn't sure if they had understood me and I repeated what I had said. They looked at each other and Adela nodded. There didn't seem much else to say and we went back to the house.

'They weren't exactly welcoming, were they?' I said.

'Well, they don't know what to expect with two foreigners turning up to live opposite them. Their lives probably haven't changed for generations and for all they know we'll be having drunken orgies and wild parties, with music blaring until early morning.'

'I certainly hope so,' I said.

'But when they find out that all we want to do is lead a quiet, simple life like them, they'll be fine.'

'Sounds a bit dull. Can't we have just one or two wild parties?'

We drove back through Spain without being stopped by the police and the official at the ferry terminal in Santander allowed the truck on to the boat without comment. Immediately we arrived back in Bristol, we put our house on the market. It took three months to sell, and the young couple who bought it told us that they were going to remove the carrots and parsnips from the flowerbeds in the front garden and replace the lawns in the back. We gave our chickens and rabbits to two of my work colleagues and sold what little furniture we had left.

Everyone we knew in Bristol came to our leaving party. There were genteel ladies from Linda's painting group; *aficionados* of Spain from our evening classes; friends of mine from work and tennis; an assortment of neighbours, who referred to us as hippies; and Linda's boss. He brought along a tall, exotic woman who had dyed her hair maroon and stained her legs the same colour. Everyone brought booze and crowded into our kitchen, with its trendy orange bench tops and burnt-orange floor tiles, spilt drinks and ate paella. Late in the evening, when the house was overflowing and people were dancing the flamenco, I asked the woman with the maroon hair how far up she had stained her legs.

She looked into my eyes and touched my chest with her long fingers. 'All the way, Barry,' she said. 'I always go all the way.'

Thinking about it still makes me tingle.

It was not yet light when, three days later, we set off in the Bedford van that, two years before, I had been uncertain would make the journey back from France. After more than twenty months of noisy and exuberant planning, our departure was an anticlimax - no fanfare, just a cold and early start. I closed and locked the front door of our first home and dropped the keys through the letterbox. Linda watched me from the van as Matt Ashford's son ghosted past on his bicycle on his way to the early shift. He called out, 'Good luck' and raised his hand without looking back.

We had a shoebox full of cards wishing us well on

our adventure, and most of our friends said that they would visit us once we had civilised the *cortijo*. My brother simply wrote, "Good luck climbing the wall."

Looking back now, I am not sure if my efforts to climb the wall arose from an overwhelming desire to find out what was on the other side - as my family believed - or whether I was simply running away.

CHAPTER FIVE

We crossed from Plymouth to Santander and drove the same route that we had taken three months before in the removal truck. Around lunchtime on the first day, we were grinding our way along a corkscrewing pass through the Cantabrian Mountains when an empty sand truck overtook us and bounced on ahead in a cloud of dust. It threw up a pebble and I watched it spiral towards us in slow motion until it struck the windscreen in front of my eyes - the glass crazed and I was blind. We were saved by the sliding doors. We hauled them open and Linda leant out and watched for traffic in front while I looked down at a six feet strip of road alongside me and tried to keep the wheels on the tarmac, away from the unfenced edge and a very long drop. It took forever to brake to a halt, and all the while Linda was screaming out, 'It's all clear ahead! Keep it straight! There's nothing in front!'

After I had pulled on the handbrake, we sat and held each other before I climbed down on wobbly legs and hacked away the glass with the wheel brace. We were happy to be alive and the loss of the windscreen was a minor inconvenience, but we did not know that we would be driving for the next two years without it. Two days later, eighty miles from Los Sanchez, we were pulled over by two motorcycle cops. They were wearing brown leather jackets and mirror sunglasses. The younger one stood by their bikes as the older one approached us, unsmiling. I stood alongside the van and waited for him.

'It is illegal to drive without a windscreen,' he said.

I had driven a long way and I was tired. 'Why? Your motorbikes don't have windscreens.'

His face stiffened. 'Because it is the law of Spain.'

I unwisely pointed out that our van without its windscreen was no different to a Jeep with a wind-down windscreen, a moped, a bicycle, a motorcycle, a tractor, or - stretching the point - a convertible sports car, all of which were legal.

He unbuttoned the top pocket of his jacket and took out his notebook. 'Passport, driver's licence and insurance, *por favor.*'

Linda climbed down from the van, adjusted her skirt, and joined us. The policeman who had stayed with the motorcycles had been watching her. He took off his helmet, placed it on the seat of his bike, and walked over, rearranging his hair with his hands. He smiled at Linda.

She smiled back. 'We didn't know it was the law of Spain and we're very sorry,' she said. 'It's only just happened and we're going to replace the windscreen as soon as we get to a large town.'

I rummaged in the van and came out with our document folder, but the policeman had put away his notebook. They were discussing with Linda the best place to buy a windscreen for a foreign vehicle. They agreed that, because of the age of our van, it might prove to be difficult and we would probably have to drive to Granada. Linda thanked them for their help and shook their hands as she said goodbye. The policemen watched Linda closely as she climbed up into the van and returned her waves as we drove off.

Linda turned to me. 'I think, in future, you'd better let me handle these situations.'

'Suits me,' I said. 'Just don't wear jeans.'

In Granada we were told that the windscreen would have to be flown out from England and would cost the equivalent of our budget for ten week's living expenses - and was more than the van was worth. We drove on without ordering it and were stopped twenty miles further on by two policemen in a van. We explained that the windscreen could not be purchased in Spain and we would have to wait until we went back to England. They spoke together briefly and waved us on. This was to be our reply on many occasions until the local police came to know us and the van, and looked away when we drove past.

We turned off the main road before Castell and took the short cut through to the *rambla* that we had discovered three months before. The narrow track goes past the warehouses of the *cooperativo,* where the locally grown fruit and vegetables are marketed, and rows of modern refrigerated trucks destined for northern Europe wait in orderly rows. We pulled over for an ancient, wooden-sided truck heading for the *cooperativo,* piled high with water melons and belching black smoke. We drove past plastic greenhouses and the chemical smells of fertilisers; past the thump of the diesel motors that drive the pumps of the bores; past piles of tattered yellowing plastic that had been stripped from the greenhouses and was waiting to be burnt - until finally we emerged on to the open expanse of the *rambla*. The workers in the fields looked up to watch the van. We waved but they were unresponsive. They didn't know us; to them we were just tourists passing through.

We pulled off the *rambla* into the *barranco* below Los Sanchez, walked up the front path, and inspected our home. José had planted the field with a full battalion of *habichuelas* and the first tendrils were starting to feel their way up the tripods; the orange and mandarin trees were laden with green fruit; and there was a potato mountain in an outhouse. Mice had made a nest in the settee; rats had gnawed a box of candles and chewed away the cover and most of the inside of a golf ball, exposing a mass of stringy elastic and an indeterminate hard, grey substance – but, otherwise, nothing had altered since June. Opposite in Los Morales, Adela stood on her balcony and watched as we unloaded the van and carried suitcases and boxes up the path. I waved and called across to her, '*Hola!*' She returned my wave and continued to watch us.

The news of our arrival spread fast and half-an-hour later we heard a hollow cough and José materialised on the terrace. He took the cigarette out of his mouth, shook our hands, and launched into a barrage of Spanish.

'*No comprendo,*' said Linda, 'speak more slowly.'

José started again at a marginally reduced pace,

before quickly accelerating to his normal speed. I made out that he was welcoming us and telling us that he was an honest man and we were now part of his family. He made an expansive gesture at the rows of beans. 'Half are yours,' he said and led us to the pile of potatoes. 'These are all yours.'

There appeared to be a year's supply of potatoes in the outhouse and when the beans came into production they would feed a decent-sized town. 'No, José, you grew them; you sell them. We'll just take enough to eat.'

After José left, we took stock of the situation. Half the farmhouse was in reasonable condition and we would set this up as our temporary living quarters while we carried out the renovations to the remainder. All the rooms were tiny, although some had started off a reasonable size, but in the recent past they had been partitioned with flimsy brick walls. None of the rooms had doors, just low openings that were at forehead height for Linda and nose height for me. Until we became used to them, there were regular thuds followed by screams or swearing. For days, we walked around with bruised faces and our shoulders hunched in defensive stoops. I am sure our neighbours thought we spent the evenings fighting each other.

The largest room had just enough space for our double bed and a single wardrobe, and the lounge for two armchairs and a coffee table. We turned the front room into the kitchen/dining-room, with a sink and a small pine table, and this room doubled as the bathroom. We covered the remainder of our furniture with plastic sheeting and stacked it downstairs in the semi-ruined section. The only place for a chemical toilet was in the low-ceilinged attic, which was reached by a narrow, stone staircase of extraordinary steepness, with each step having a gargantuan riser. The steps were the only large thing about the house and Linda approached them like a rock climber. For her, each trip to the toilet was a reluctant adventure.

The entire house had a sickly, waxy smell that had impregnated the mattresses and the upholstery of our furniture during the three months it had been stored there. We learnt from José that, prior to electricity being installed along the *rambla* eight years before, all the houses had been lit with lamps that burned rendered pig fat. Over the decades, the smoke had penetrated deep into the walls and ceilings and, despite the annual coats of whitewash, the oily residue permeated through. The house was built into the side of a hill and even in summer the back walls were cool and had a slightly damp odour. The combined smells of must and tallow gave the farmhouse a highly distinctive character.

A few days after we arrived, a new Land-Rover pulled up in the *barranco* and out bounced a young, freckled-faced Canadian named Benny. He had bought a large house in Ferrer, an abandoned village several miles away, and having heard that we had moved into the area had come over to check us out. Benny was married to the daughter of an English couple who had also bought a *cortijo* nearby, and we learnt that several other foreigners had purchased properties in the area, mostly for holiday homes. Carlos Risueño had been very busy in the twenty-two months since we bought

Los Sanchez.

The road to Ferrer led off the *rambla* and was two miles of horseshoe bends up a steep, rutted earth track that was impassable after heavy rain – nonetheless, Benny had grand plans for his property. He was returning to Canada to earn some money and, when he came back to Ferrer, was going to convert his house into a bar and have live music to attract the youth for miles around. The geographical unsuitability of the location, together with the fact that Ferrer had no electricity, did not appear to have occurred to him or, if it had, was not going to deter him. Benny had been living in Ferrer for several months and handled himself with confidence forged from the experience. He was street smart and assured, and had no trouble negotiating his way through complex situations. His Spanish was no better than ours, but he was dismissive of this limitation.

'If you don't know the word, just use English and stick an "o" on the end,' he said. 'It works ninety percent of the time.'

So, his conversations went something like: '*Hola, Antonio, mañana* goingo *arriba el* hillo to *comprar vino* and hamo.' Which, translated, meant, 'Hallo, Antonio, tomorrow I'm going up the hill to buy some wine and ham.' Inexplicably, they seemed to understand him, but, whenever we tried it, all we got were faces screwed up in disbelief.

Like us, Benny had found out that the locals had unlimited time to talk about the weather, their crops and the juicy local gossip, and when they ran out of conversation they would simply stand and smile at us.

They were unused to our culture where we perpetually tore around doing important tasks. We were anxious not to offend anyone and we had resigned ourselves to spending a large part of our days engaged in desultory conversations interspersed with companionable silences, but Benny had discovered the polite way to terminate these conversations.

'You just say *bueno*,' he told us. 'As soon as you say *bueno*, everybody understands you've got something better to do than stand around all day talking crap, and you don't upset anyone.'

Literally, *bueno* means good, but when it is said with a degree of finality it means that the speaker wants to terminate the conversation. As we became more experienced with the word, we began to see subtle variations in its use. We watched as conversations naturally ran down and the pauses grew longer. Eventually, one of the speakers would give, with obvious reluctance, a long drawn out *bueno*, almost a sigh, which conveyed to the listener that the speaker would like, above all else, to spend the whole day talking about nothing, and it was with much regret that he had to take his leave in order to do something trivial but unavoidable, like going off to work in the *campo* picking beans. Then there was the firm, decisive *bueno* that was said immediately after the compulsory questions about family and before the conversation had got into its stride. There was no mistaking this. It signalled the immediate end to the conversation. The speaker was on a mission and there would be no dilly-dallying today. The most confusing *bueno* was when it was spoken without inflection in a short break in a conversation, generally after a topic had been dealt with to the point of exhaustion. The speaker would say nothing further but show no sign of departing. After many months of trying to decipher this message we decided that when the speaker could think of nothing else to say, but wasn't yet ready to leave, it was said as a prompt for the listener to start on a new subject, and roughly translated meant - I feel that I ought to sound as if I've got something else to do, even though I haven't, so if you can think of anything to talk about at all, however uninteresting, it will give me a good reason to stay and chat for a while longer.

Spanish is a logical language and one of the easiest to learn. With the exception of the letters 'h', and 'u' when it follows 'q' - both of which are silent - every letter is pronounced and the rules of pronunciation are consistent, although if you are not accustomed to this it can cause major confusion. When a couple started talking to us about Shack-ess-pay-ar-ay, we asked them five times to repeat it. They were clearly having difficulty understanding how two people could be so badly educated that they had not heard of their own country's most famous writer, when it finally dawned on us that this is the Spanish pronunciation of Shakespeare. We had a similar experience with the Bay-at-less and it wasn't until they said John, Paul, George and Ringo that we knew who they were talking about. But, after you get used to this, Spanish is really quite straightforward.

English, on the other hand, with its eccentric spelling and varying pronunciations, is a nightmare for everyone. A Spaniard who attempts to learn English is, at some stage, faced with the appalling OUGH. He is told the different pronunciations of this unlikely collection of letters in words such as: through, thorough, thought, though, trough, and bough. Confronted with this insanity, the average Spaniard asks himself how Sir Francis Drake, or in actual fact Drack-ay, could possibly have defeated the Armada and resolves to take up Japanese instead.

Spanish, in theory, does not have these pitfalls. That is, until you go somewhere like rural Andalucía. In our region, they had decided to economise on syllables and largely do away with the letter S. Words such as *mercado* (market) became *m'cow*; the village *Castell* was *Catay*; and *dos* (two) was *do*. If we pronounced the word *tres* (three) correctly and asked for three bottles of wine, we were given *trece* (thirteen). I began to seriously wonder if we were in Spain at all, or whether we had taken a wrong turn in Madrid and ended up in Portugal. It took us several months to embrace this new language and for us to understand the locals and, in turn, be understood. Inexplicably, they found the pronunciation of Barry impossible. Nearly half the women in the region were called Mari-Carmen and I explained that all they had to do was substitute a B for the M and drop the Carmen and *eso es* - that's it! But they never quite managed it and the closest they came sounded uncannily like *all-i-oli* - a sauce made from garlic and olive oil. Of course, they had absolutely no problem with Linda, which is a Spanish word meaning pretty that locally they pronounced *Yinda*. Consequently we were referred to as *Yinda* and the husband. After several months, I came to accept my subordinate status, realizing it was better than being called Garlic Sauce.

CHAPTER SIX

The farmhouse had been unoccupied for many years and an assortment of squatters had moved in. A pair of swallows came and went through the holes in the roof and had made a nest against a rafter. The floor beneath was littered with their droppings and feathers. They were unconcerned by our arrival and continued to roost in the house for several months. After we repaired the roof, they moved to our bedroom and flew in and out through the window. We closed the shutters at night and, if we didn't open them at first light, the swallows became increasingly restless and eventually made forays around the house looking for another way out.

The floor of our bedroom was a thin layer of crumbling concrete over earth. On our second night in the room Linda heard scratching and pattering and, deciding that it was something I ought to deal with, woke me up. I shone the torch around, but neither heard nor saw anything. The next night I was quicker. Spotlighted in the beam, I saw the well-rounded hairy bottom and bootlace tail of a rat disappearing down a hole near the bed. It was 2 am, the time when I am least capable of dealing with these situations. Also, I was in my pyjamas in a warm bed; my shoes were by the kitchen door; and it occurred to me that there could be a lot of other nasty things out there. Mice are just a nuisance, but rats are big enough to inflict damage - I remembered what they'd done to my golf ball. They also spread truly horrible diseases like bubonic plague and, for all I knew, rabies and smallpox. I turned over. No, this was definitely best left until morning.

Linda elbowed me. 'Do something. Quickly, before it comes back.'

I managed to get from the bedroom to the kitchen by climbing over pieces of furniture and my feet only touched the floor twice. I returned with a plastic bucket, which I placed upside down over the hole. I thought about it and went back to the kitchen for two heavy cookbooks that I put on top of the bucket. For the rest of the night we lay awake listening to the rat running round and round inside the bucket. When grey light eventually filtered through the shutters, I got out of bed and cemented up the hole.

After dark, the house became the domain of the geckos. During the day, they hid and slept among the rafters and, after we hung up pictures and mirrors, some took up residence behind them. They began to call to each other about an hour after sunset, a gentle chek ... chek, while they remained out of sight. It was their signal to come out to hunt and for us to leave. If we stayed in the room, they started to get impatient and their calls became harsh and scolding until, finally, a large male would show himself and shriek at us from a rafter, like an irate parent telling his children to go to bed. They hunted in our bedroom, hanging off the cane ceiling, leaping to catch moths in mid air before landing on our bed. Occasionally, two males fought. The fights were ferocious and swift, and ended with the vanquished in full flight, sometimes minus his tail, being pursued by the victor.

'A house without geckos is an unlucky house,' said José. 'You are fortunate to have so many. It means you will have lots of good luck.'

Lucky they might have been, but many nights they interrupted our sleep and right then we would have settled for just a couple of geckos and a little less luck.

We had mice in their dozens and some days we emptied the same traps four or five times. They made nests under the roof tiles, inside cupboard drawers and cushions, and in the saddle bag of my bike - which I discovered one day when they jumped out as I wheeled it down the path. We stored all our food in containers and checked our shoes before we put them on. It took several weeks to eradicate them, but not before they had attracted snakes. The first time that we saw a snake inside the house we were in the tiny, temporary lounge. I noticed flakes of whitewash drifting down from the cane ceiling and looked up. A slim, three-foot-long snake had coiled itself around a mouse and was hanging from a beam. It had come under the roof tiles and through a gap between the canes. The problem was, now that it was wrapped around the mouse, it was too large to go back. We sidled out of the room and stood in the doorway to the kitchen looking up at it. It tried again to get through the gap and brought down more whitewash.

'What on earth are we going to do?'

'We could go into Castell for a drink and hope it's gone when we get back, or alternatively I could try to knock it down with a stick and shove it out of the door.'

The issue resolved itself when the mouse wriggled free and scurried along the beam, before darting into a hole at the top of the wall. The snake failed to realise that it had lost its prey and continued to coil itself around an imaginary mouse. When it finally discovered that all it was constricting was its own body, it gave us a snaky look and disappeared back through the opening in the cane ceiling.

The second snake incident took place in our bedroom, in the early hours of the morning. At this stage, an uninterrupted night's sleep was a thing of the past and, when Linda nudged me, I was instantly alert, like a well-trained commando.

'There's something up there ... not a gecko.'

I pointed the torch at the ceiling and turned it on. Directly above the bed a snake was dangling from a beam. Its shadow against the whitewashed cane ceiling made it appear enormous. Linda screamed; I shouted; and the snake curled itself back and vanished into a hole where a section of cane was missing. I fetched two hurricane lamps from the kitchen and we kept a vigil until morning, when I mixed up a bucket of plaster and filled every gap between the canes, down to the tiniest crevice.

A few years before, while we were living in Australia, we heard numerous stories of snakes crawling into campers' sleeping bags, attracted by the warmth. During the night, the rightful occupant had rolled over on to the snake and promptly been bitten. I was convinced that this snake had been heading directly for our bed and, if Linda hadn't woken up, it would have snuggled in between us. That must have been what José meant about the geckos bringing good luck.

The electricity line ran up the *rambla* from Castell and stopped opposite us at Los Morales. At the end of the line the level of power was atrocious. It was too feeble to operate a room heater or even an electric kettle and, when homes down-line used an appliance, the lights in Los Morales flickered and dimmed. Very few homes had a television and some, like ours, had not had electricity connected. No one had a telephone and many houses did not have running water. Los Morales had two families who were permanent residents, although at one time there had been four other families in the hamlet, but they had either died or moved away. Fra'quito and Adela lived in the centre of Los Morales and their balcony looked directly across at our terrace. They had four children: Antonio, who was married and worked as a *mulero*; Pepe, who had just completed his national service in the army; Little Adela, who was 16 and engaged to an older man from a nearby village; and Miguelito, who boarded during the week at a high school 25 miles away. He was intelligent and the family had hopes that he would go to university in Granada and become an engineer. In deference to his superior brain power, Miguelito was excused from working in the fields when he came home at the weekends and, instead, he stayed inside listening to pop music.

The other residents of Los Morales were Bernardo and Carmela, an older couple with no children, who lived at the highest point alongside the road leading to the mountain village of Rubité. The two families lived less than thirty yards apart, but they had not spoken for decades. We had watched Bernardo and Fra'quito squeeze past each other on the narrow path outside their houses, with set faces and no acknowledgement that the other existed. If it had not been for the simultaneous sideways movement of each man as they passed, it was as if the other were invisible. Benny told us he had heard that the feud started in the Civil War when the two families became divided by different loyalties. Bernardo had fought on the side of the government and the communists, and Fra'quito's father and uncles for the rebel fascists. When we asked José, he said that this was romantic nonsense and the families had fallen out over the boundaries of their land. Manuel, from La Venta, disagreed with José and said that the argument had been about water rights, or else it was over the repayment of a loan, but he couldn't recall which; it was all too long ago. No one could remember any more - including probably Bernardo and Fra'quito.

'Only one thing is certain,' said José, smiling, 'the feud was not about love. In those days we worked so hard we were too tired to fight over women.'

Our first weeks there were unreal; it was as though we had been transported to a parallel world. We were isolated by a different culture and language, which excluded us from the world we saw going on around us. To the locals, we were a diversion - an early taste of reality TV. The two families in Los Morales stood on their balconies and watched us for hours as we carried out the most mundane of tasks. Men dismounted from their mules and tethered them in the *barranco*, and *campesinos* in the surrounding fields paused in their work and leant on their mattocks, as they uniformly gazed up at our terrace. Passing motorists on the Rubité road stopped their vehicles and whole families got out to stare across at our house. José had the habit of appearing silently at any time of the day, but unfailingly at the most inconvenient moment and with no definable reason for his visit, announcing himself with his diplomatic, sheep's cough. Men we had never seen before came into our field and stood looking up at us, not twenty-five paces away. If we waved, they didn't respond. They were spectators, not participants, in this drama. One day Linda and I performed an impromptu jive on our terrace, but no one applauded. It was the type of odd thing that foreigners were expected to do, or perhaps it was just that we were awful at jiving.

One day I caused consternation by washing out a pair of jeans and hanging them on a line I'd strung between two trees. I sensed a flurry of movement from the balconies opposite and saw that the spectators had moved to better vantage points. There were designated roles for men and women and I had upset the natural order of things. Men did not do the washing. They ploughed fields; planted crops; pruned fruit trees; cleaned out water deposits and irrigation channels; and smoked and drank copious amounts. Women raised the children; cooked and washed; looked after the chickens; helped pick the crops; whitewashed their houses inside and out once a year; and remained sober and respectable. Linda broke the rules of female behaviour by helping me mix cement, render walls, and clamber on roofs to replace tiles, and she regularly drank beer and wine in public – and in significant quantities, I might add.

Through us, the people had a window into a culture that was as new to them as theirs was to us, but when they discovered that we didn't dance naked or have orgies on the terrace, and their women and children were safe from moral corruption - that, in fact, our lives were no more interesting than their own - the novelty of watching us wore off. But they were intrigued by the way we swapped what they considered were clearly defined gender roles. One day, Little Adela called over from Los Morales and saw me cutting up vegetables for the evening meal.

She spoke to Linda about it. 'In your country, do the men do the cooking as well as the washing?'

'Well, it's changing,' said Linda. 'If the man goes out to work all day and the woman stays at home looking after the children, then normally she would do the cooking and washing. Nowadays, though, a lot of couples both go out to work and it isn't fair that the woman should do all the housework, so they share it.'

Little Adela thought about it and nodded. The faintest stirrings of feminism were being felt in southern Spain.

We were also doing tasks that the locals left to tradesmen. The men did no work to their houses other than the most basic maintenance; instead they employed *albanils,* handymen builders with modest skills, whose daily rate was little better than a *campesino.* But even that was more than we could afford. The majority of the immediate work we had to do was not complicated: rebuilding stone walls, repairing internal render, cementing floors, and building stone steps. We could see no point in spending our meagre budget on work we could do ourselves. In this part of Spain the houses had been built simply and cheaply, wherever possible using materials that cost nothing. Stones for the walls had been collected from the *rambla,* and earth was sieved and made into mud to bind the stones. Many of the floors were compacted earth, some with home-made clay tiles or flat stones embedded into the earth, or with a thin slurry of cement on top. The rafters, beams and joists were made from straight branches cut from white cedar and eucalyptus trees, and bamboo canes were used for the ceilings. None of the windows had glass and the openings were small. The houses did not have bathrooms and if they had running water it was from a single tap in the kitchen, connected by hosepipe plumbing. The only expensive items were the doors, the window shutters and the terracotta roof tiles. Higher into the mountains, they had been too poor to afford the tiles and their houses had flat roofs made of mud. They added a fresh layer each year in the spring, stamping it with their bare feet, and then let the summer sun bake it until it became like concrete. It kept the rain out for twelve months before they had to do it again.

Inside our house, the floors sloped, not one of the

walls was straight, and the render that still remained on the walls had great swirls and lumps. This was my type of building - primitive, functional, and could be done rapidly. It mattered little if my walls curved and the floors had dips, or if the render I slapped on was rough or smooth - it simply matched the rest of the house. But the collapsed and damaged sections of roof were beyond me; I needed an *albanil* to show me what to do. The roofs were built in the traditional manner – white cedar rafters with bamboo canes laid crossways and a layer of mud on top, into which the roof tiles were bedded. José introduced me to an *albanil* from a nearby hamlet and I employed him to replace the partially collapsed section of roof above the room that would become our lounge. It took the *albanil* and his assistant three days to demolish the remains of the old roof and then rebuild it, while I helped - sieving earth, mixing mud, and ferrying materials up the ladder. It was reminiscent of my days as the bottom hand for the scaffolders in Bristol, and I had the same trouble understanding the *albanil's* instructions - but in those three days I learnt the skills to repair the other roofs.

I became an expert at demolishing walls. I discovered it was much easier to knock down a wall than to build one, and far more enjoyable. I first took the sledgehammer to the brick partition walls in the kitchen and lounge, and within the space of a day I doubled the size of the two rooms. The main walls of the house were a more serious proposition. I needed to make openings for doors and windows, but the walls were two feet thick, built from stones and mud, and many were load-bearing. I felt that if I wielded the

sledgehammer with the same Thor-like vigour that I
had attacked the partition walls I was likely to bring the
house down. The stone walls required caution, as well
as a more scientific approach. I decided to conduct a
few trials and start off in a modest way by raising the
height of the existing doorways. It was also a pressing
job; we were tired of limboing our way from room to
room and nearly knocking ourselves unconscious in
moments of forgetfulness. I calculated that I needed to
chisel out the stones and mud to half the thickness of
wall at the required height above the door opening,
then insert a timber lintel to support the wall above,
and afterwards do the same to the wall on the other
side of the opening. It would then be safe to knock out
the section of wall beneath the lintels, without ending
up buried under a ton of stones, mud and roof tiles. At
my first attempt, each time I removed a stone from the
wall I leapt backwards and stood at a safe distance,
scanning the surrounding area for signs of cracking and
listening for ominous creaking - but the theory worked
and no walls collapsed. Afterwards, it was wonderful to
walk around the house without ducking and dodging
and our bruises began to fade away. Buoyed with these
successes, I graduated to smashing openings for
windows and doorways by using the same principal of
first inserting lintels into the wall above the opening. I
installed a window above the kitchen sink and made
doorways to connect two outhouses to the main house -
an old mule stable that was earmarked to become a
bedroom, and the store room off the terrace, where
José had kept the potato mountain. As I was making
the openings, I discovered that the mud between the

stones was honeycombed with tunnels and I came across the bodies of mice and rats, entombed deep inside the walls in hollowed out nests lined with straw and leaves - ancient, odourless bodies that someone, decades before, had sealed in. It seemed a shame to disturb them after so long.

At the beginning, much of our time was taken up with water - something in England we had never thought about. You turned on a tap and out it poured. You removed a plug and away it went. But here, it ruled our lives. We filled containers by siphoning water from the irrigation channel that ran alongside the front of the house on its way to neighbouring fields, and we had a line of buckets, bowls and two watering cans against the kitchen wall. Then, after we used the water, we had to get rid of it. We couldn't pour it down the kitchen sink to find its way into a drain. There *was* no drainage system. For a week we lived with a large bucket under the sink to catch the waste water. It needed emptying three or four times a day and occasionally we forgot and dirty water flooded the floor. It became our number one priority and, watched by our neighbours, I dug a large hole in the field, filled it with rocks, ran a pipe into it from the sink outlet and covered the hole. We still had to carry the water in, but at least we didn't have to carry it out again.

We owned a one tenth share of the irrigation water, which came from a swimming-pool-sized deposit into which the *barranco* had been diverted. The short section of irrigation channel directly outside our house was lined with concrete, but the remainder was earth

71

and the water carried with it fine particles of soil, which settled if it was left to stand. We had brought an electric pump from England and I had decided that the simplest method of installing running water was to site our two tanks on the hillside above Los Sanchez, pump the water up to them from the channel and then gravity feed it into the house. The *barranco* was fed by springs and gullies in the mountains and, apart from the goats and sheep that drank in it upstream, was unpolluted - or so we had thought until at first light one morning we were awakened by voices close to the house. I pulled on my satin kimono and went outside to investigate. Four women wearing headscarfs were standing about twenty feet from our front door using the water in the channel to do their washing. They were chatting and laughing and each had a substantial plastic basket filled with laundry. I watched as the women spread wet towels out on to three massive stone slabs that spanned the channel. They rubbed the towels with round detergent blocks, pounded them against the stones a few times and then rinsed them in the passing water. We had previously wondered at the purpose of these slabs, but it had never once occurred to us that they were washing stones.

I didn't recognise any of the women and when they noticed me they fell silent. I drew my kimono tighter and mumbled, '*Buenos dias,*' before going inside to tell Linda.

'We seem to have acquired the local Laundromat. There's a bunch of women outside and they're polluting the channel. We can't pump up water full of their suds.'

'Well it's hardly important because right now we

don't have electricity to do any pumping. When we do, we'll ask them nicely if they'll do their washing down-channel.'

We never needed to ask them. After several more laundry sessions the women stopped coming. They were clearly uncomfortable doing their washing at Los Sanchez now that we were in residence. We later discovered that each hamlet and village had a communal wash-area. They were part of the community life, a meeting place for the women where they could escape from their houses, complain about their husbands and spread scurrilous gossip. It was more time consuming than throwing the washing into a machine, but considerably more enjoyable. Several weeks later, I drove past the row of concrete laundry troughs at La Venta and saw the four women who had used the washing stones outside our house. I waved and they smiled back.

The water in the channel was not clean enough for drinking or cooking and for the first few weeks we drove to the service station in Castell and used their tap to fill two five-gallon plastic barrels that, in Bristol, I had used for making beer. When José found out what we were doing, he dismissed the Castell water as poisonous and told us about a spring of pure water much closer by in the hills behind La Venta. He gave me directions, which involved driving a short distance along the road to Ferrer and then branching off on foot for about fifty yards. It sounded straightforward and I arrived at the spot expecting to find a clear pool, or a spring welling out of the ground, or at least *some* evidence of water. But there was none, just a smooth

73

rock face at the foot of a steep slope. The track ended here and I concluded that this must pass for humour in Andalucía - a person asks for water, so you send him to a rock. I recalled that Moses had managed to produce water in similar circumstances, but in the absence of a suitable staff I abandoned the idea.

On the way back, I saw José near Los Morales and stopped the van. I walked towards him swinging the two beer barrels and laughing to show that I appreciated his joke. After five minutes of misunderstanding, during which José tried his hardest to see why two empty barrels were so amusing and must have thought I was certifiable, he went with me back to the rock face and pointed. I looked, but saw nothing - just rock with what looked like a root growing out of it. José's face broke into a smile; he reached forward, pulled out the gnarled piece of wood and a jet of water followed. The rock formed a natural chamber in which water collected after being filtered through countless layers. It was probably the purest water in the whole of Spain and here it was, five minutes from our house up a dusty track. In other countries they would have built a bottling factory and sold it as a cure for things like dyspepsia and melancholy.

Much later, we brought our visiting friends to the spring as part of their tourist itinerary. Of course, they always spotted straight away that you pulled out the bung to release the water.

CHAPTER SEVEN

During our first week at the house, two *guardia civil* arrived on motorbikes. Theirs were not the fast bikes of the highway cops who'd spotted the broken windscreen and stopped us on the way down, but were low-powered bikes for pottering around the towns, and would have given them a slow and bumpy ride up the *rambla*. It was nine o'clock in the morning and I was cementing up cracks in the outside wall. I put down the trowel and called to Linda. Whenever I see a policeman, I have an irrational sense of guilt and do a mental check of anything I might have done wrong. Whatever it was, for two *guardia civil* to come to the house, it must have been bad. During Franco's dictatorship, the *guardia civil* earned a reputation for brutality that made them feared throughout Spain. I had encountered them on two previous occasions some years before; once when I was leaving the beach at Blanes, without a shirt, and another time when I was walking on a beach alongside the border with Gibraltar. That was in the days when the border was closed and I had strayed too close to it for their liking. Both times I had a sub-machine gun poked in my face.

We stood together on the terrace and watched apprehensively as they walked up the front path, but the policemen were smiling and at pains to reassure us. It was *muy normal,* simply a matter of routine; the *guardia* always visit new people who move into their district. We had not yet registered with any of the authorities and no one except our neighbours knew we had arrived. Franco had been dead for four years, but his spy network was alive and well. I invited them to sit at the table on the terrace.

'Would you like coffee?' I said.

They looked severe, shook their heads and tutted. It was as though I'd offered them a bribe.

'Some *vino*?' said Linda.

They shook their heads again, but less emphatically and they didn't tut.

'Some *coñac*?' I said.

They looked at their watches. *'Si, un poco coñac, bueno.'*

They stayed for more than an hour and the four of us drank cognac. They wanted to know what work we would be doing; how we would earn enough to live. We were not legally entitled to work in Spain - the Spanish government was happy for foreigners to buy property and bring money into the country, but they didn't want them to work and take Spaniards' jobs. We told them that we were renovating the *cortijo* and working on the land, nothing else. We had invested the money from the sale of our house in England and were living on the proceeds. The two *guardia* must have decided we weren't a threat to anyone and lost interest in us. They devoted their attention to the cognac and talked about themselves. They were from Valencia and Murcia and lived in the *cuartel* - the barracks in Castell. It was a good posting, very little crime and it was peaceful, except in summer when the tourists came. They became jovial and made jokes that we laughed at, but didn't understand. They admired our *cortijo* and the land, and posed for photographs with Linda, letting her try on their black patent-leather *tricornio* hats. When the litre bottle of cognac was empty they left.

As soon as they had gone, Linda went back to bed and I wondered whether it was compulsory to be an alcoholic to live here. I picked up the bucket of hardening cement and reeled about, randomly slapping it on anything that looked as though it deserved it, before I staggered upstairs to join Linda.

We had been there for only a few weeks when Benny went back to Canada. We missed him. He was full of enthusiasm and his advice to us had been invaluable. Just before he left he told us about a bar in La Venta that he had visited during the summer. We drove past La Venta on our trips up and down the *rambla*, but we had never seen a sign.

'It's not legit,' said Benny. 'They don't have *documentacion*, so they don't advertise they're there. You just hear about it.'

'Knock twice and ask for Paco?' I said.

Benny smiled. 'Sort of, but you ask for Fra'quito El Bar.'

An illicit bar; it was irresistible. This was the real Spain. Not a tourist bar selling English beer and playing *Viva España* through a loudspeaker. I pictured the hip youth of the region hanging out there. Long-haired Spaniards sitting in dark corners, moodily plucking the strings of their guitars; and beautiful girls, with gypsy faces and gold hoop earrings, flamenco dancing in guttering candle light; and *sangria* and *Cuba libre* flowing unchecked. The night we visited the bar we dressed in our trendiest clothes. Linda wore a multi-coloured peasant skirt, a semi-transparent cheesecloth top, and strings of coloured beads. I had on flared emerald-green velvet trousers and a cream silk shirt with blouson sleeves and most of its buttons undone. We looked extraordinarily cool.

The evening was still and warm and we decided to walk down the *rambla* to La Venta. We knew where Fra'quito El Bar lived and, as we had expected, his door was closed, although we could hear noises coming from inside. I knocked twice and after a few moments the door partly opened and Fra'quito El Bar's bristly face appeared. He seemed surprised to see us and he held on to the door with one hand. '*Qué?*'

'We've come for a drink,' I said.

'A drink?' said Fra'quito and thought about it. 'Okay, come in.'

The bar was the front room of his house. The only light was from a television set and there were three rows of hard, wooden chairs in front of it, like a miniature cinema. I made out the slumped figures of some of our neighbours, still in their work clothes. They looked at us briefly, before returning to the screen, and I moved further into the room to see what they were watching. It was *Starsky and Hutch* - in black and white. Unfortunately, there were a couple of spare seats and, feeling ridiculous, we stayed three quarters of an hour, drank warm beer, and endured a badly-dubbed episode of *Starsky and Hutch* - which managed to make all the characters, regardless of whether they were male or female, sound exactly the same. But, the worst thing was, we'd seen it.

We left the bar and walked back up the *rambla*. 'Benny must be a *Starsky and Hutch* fan,' Linda giggled. I started imitating the wooden dubbing and, by the time we reached Los Sanchez, we were in hysterics. Three days later, a police van called at La Venta and the bar never opened again.

'Well, that's it, then,' I said, 'no more wild nightlife.'

We were starting to get to know our neighbours and, through José Manzano, we met the three sisters and their families who lived in La Venta. Their houses were in a small group, set slightly apart from the rest of the hamlet, and they shared a huge vine-covered terrace that looked down onto the *rambla*. José's cousin, *primo* Agosto, had married the youngest of the sisters, Francesca, and they had a quiet, serious son, Antonio. José took us to their house when we were trying to find roof tiles to replace the hundreds that were missing or broken. Behind his house, *primo* Agosto had a large stack of tiles that he'd salvaged from a derelict outhouse and we offered to buy them from him.

'Come down with your van and take what you need,' he said.

'But how much do you want for them?'

He looked at José. 'You're friends of my *primo*,' he

79

said. 'They're a *regalo*.'

'We can't accept them as a gift,' I said.

He smiled. 'You will have to, if you want them.'

This was typical of the kindness of the three families, and of many people in the area. For generations they had been poor, but they were generous with what little they did have and they wanted nothing in return. There was no debt that we would be reminded of and asked to repay at a distant point in the future.

The middle sister, Madelena, was married to Francisco. His nickname was *Alcalde* - which means mayor. He had never been the mayor, but he had an aura of wisdom and honesty and people turned to him if ever there was a dispute. As well as owning a plastic greenhouse and several fields near us, he was also the area's water diviner. He used a small brass ball on a fine chain, which he carried with him in a leather pouch. I have watched him hold the chain and gently swing the ball in a circle, and seen the ball, when it came to rest, pull at an angle of 45 degrees towards the water. He and Madelena had two children, the younger, Mari-Carmen, was bubbly and beautiful and, two years before as a 15 year old, remembered Linda and I trudging up the *rambla*, with our bright orange backpacks and big hiking boots, to look at the house we had just bought - and still laughed about it. She was engaged to Paco, a truck driver for the *cooperativo*, who spent his days collecting the produce from the growers. Her brother, also called Paco, worked the fields and the greenhouse with his father and had the same air of solid dependability. Madelena was kind, matronly and tired from a life of hard work, but when she smiled the years dropped away and you saw where Mari-Carmen's beauty came from.

A few weeks after we moved in, we noticed that Francisco *Alcalde* had started to check the irrigation channel between the deposit and his field on the evening before he used the water. He told me that he was looking for earth falls or other blockages which would make the water overflow the channel and stop it from reaching his field. 'Better to do it now,' he said, 'rather than sit in my field in the morning, waiting, and then find out I've lost half my water.'

It seemed logical, but I'd seen Bernardo release the bung from the deposit in the morning and then walk the length of the channel, as the water flowed along it, clearing any blockages as he went. Francisco *Alcalde's* route took him past the front of our house and I would hear his quiet cough as he passed our kitchen door close to dusk, just about the time, in fact, to have a pre-dinner glass of wine. I would have the bottle ready and we would sit together on the wall of the channel, the bottle and glasses between us on one of the washing stones. He talked about Winston Churchill and Adolf Hitler; about the Spanish Civil War, in which he had been too young to fight; and about how Spain would change now that Franco was dead.

'You wait and see,' he said. 'There will be drugs and crime will increase tenfold. You will no longer be able to leave your bag in the plaza and come back two hours later to find it there. The people of Spain want a democracy, but they want a democracy with the strong laws we had under Franco.'

After an hour his conversation went in a circle and he would talk about Winston Churchill again. It was about then that his son, Paco, would appear out of the gloom. He would decline my offer of wine, listen to his father for a few moments, laughingly call him a *politico fanatico,* and take him home.

The eldest sister, Virtrudes, was married to Manuel, a gentle, smiling man, who owned fields around us. Their son, Manolo, was the most handsome man in the *rambla,* with chiselled features and liquid brown eyes. He was also the shyest person in the *rambla* and stammered achingly. We quickly became friends with the three sisters and their families and Madelena said that they were adopting us as their family *inglés.* Virtrudes and Francesca had always wanted a daughter and Linda fitted perfectly - mind you, I don't think any of the sisters was particularly bothered about having another son.

It had been a month since either of us had had a shower or a bath. We had nightly strip washes in the kitchen, and we washed our hair on the terrace, with one of us pouring saucepans of water over the other's head. Swimming in the sea also helped us to keep clean, but we yearned for a long hot soak. The bath that we had brought from England was sitting upside down in the room that would eventually become our lounge, amid piles of dried mud, broken tiles and old canes, which had been knocked into the room by the *albanil* when he replaced the roof. Although it was the largest room in the house it was windowless and the only source of light was from a stable door that opened directly onto our front path.

I had a brainwave. 'Why don't we collect up all these bits of cane and have a huge bonfire to heat up water for a bath?'

'Wonderful! When shall we do it?'

'This Sunday. When I was a child, it was the day my family had its weekly bath. It was a kind of ritual, like going to church, except we cleansed our bodies instead of our souls.'

'Who was the lucky one who went first?'

'My mother - and afterwards Neil and I got in together. When we got out it was like soup, but by that time the boiler had long enough to reheat the water for my father. He was always last because of the length of time he spent in there. He had an assortment of soaps and shampoos, and bath salts and scented white blocks that he dissolved in the water to help lift the grime. Around the edge of the bath he lined up his sponge, loofah and flannel, and a variety of brushes - some with hard bristles and others with soft. He approached the whole business like an industrial cleaner. After he'd finished scrubbing and scouring, he slapped Old Spice over his face and poured brilliantine on his hair. He emerged looking like a prune and smelling like the perfume counters at Harrods.'

The following Sunday afternoon, we filled all our saucepans and kettles with water syphoned from the channel, and positioned them on trivets and bricks around a huge cane bonfire in the field. I cleared an area around the bath and laid rugs on top of the earth floor, and set up a card table with two wine glasses and a bottle of *sidra* - a type of dry, fizzy cider that was sold in champagne bottles and, if you closed your eyes and tried hard enough, you could almost convince yourself was champagne. I half filled the bath with hot water and left several large saucepans around the bonfire to top it up. Linda eased herself into the water and I poured her a glass of *sidra*. We didn't have my father's array of bath additives, so I tipped some shampoo in and then went back down to the field to make sure that the fire wasn't burning the handles off the saucepans. I left the top half of the stable door open a fraction to let in a shaft of light.

I stood by the bonfire and spent several minutes practising until I was satisfied I had achieved the right degree of hollowness and hoarseness, and I had perfected the pitch and inflection. I then crept back to the stable door and peeped through the opening. Linda was reclining languorously. She had closed her eyes and draped her hand holding the glass of *sidra* over the side of the bath.

I coughed like an asthmatic sheep and waited a few seconds before I knocked on the door and called out, '*Yinda.*' I heard water sloshing and then I slowly opened the door.

It remains one of my favourite moments of the first few weeks we were there.

CHAPTER EIGHT

The BBC World Service was our link to the outside. The short-wave reception came complete with mandatory whistles, wheezes and humming noises, together with abrupt silences when it appeared that the broadcaster had unexpectedly died in his chair. We became resigned to missing vital parts of programmes as the reception drifted in and out, but the most maddening thing was that it was never broadcast on the same wavelength for more than a few hours at a time. To this day, I am convinced that the World Service was run by someone who was high up in espionage in World War II, a man who was used to organising French resistance broadcasts from the backs of trucks, continually changing locations and wavelengths to avoid detection. I sat for hours twiddling knobs trying to find which obscure spot on the dial the World Service had decided to broadcast from that day. If there was any logic to this apparently random elusiveness, I never discovered it. Every now and then the announcer would give a carefully encrypted message: *At oh, three-twenty GMT the World Service will transmit at four painful mega-hurts, unless you're careful, in the low to medium band, gas regulo mark three ... foxtrot oven-glove Zulu over* ... or something similar. Without the BBC decoding book, it was completely meaningless. All I knew was that at some time within the next hour or two, and inevitably just as Sport's Roundup was about to come on, the transmission would go dead. I would devote the next 15 minutes feverishly attempting to relocate the World Service, only to hear Pamela Creighton say, *'... has been transferred to Manchester United for a club record fee; and that recaps the main stories* - hum whistle fart - *until the same time tomorrow, goodbye.'* - hiss burp.

The programmes on the BBC World Service were, without exception, extraordinarily good and were a lifeline to us. We avidly listened to everything, often for no other reason than to hear English being spoken, and we knew more about what was going on in the world than at any other time in our lives. There was a stirring, serialised reading of Charles Dickens' *Little Dorrit*. The powerful writing of Dickens played on our imaginations and, for weeks, we followed Little Dorrit's fortunes, barely able to wait for the next episode, picturing the unspeakable horrors that the poor girl and her family suffered - the fall from prosperity, the hardships and deprivations of the debtor's prison, no electricity, straining to read by candlelight, and washing in a bowl of cold water.

'Phew,' I said to Linda, 'thank God we're not living in *that* era.'

I listened to tantalising snippets of the astonishing test match at Headingly when Ian Botham and Bob Willis combined to give England one of the most unlikely victories over Australia. Afterwards, I ran down the front path, whooping and waving a bricklaying trowel above my head, and bumped into José. I attempted to explain the game of cricket to him and told him about the old enemy, Australia, and the battle that takes place every two years, over a period of twenty five days, between these two countries from different hemispheres - with the reward a little urn containing a smelly pile of one-hundred-year-old ashes. The more I talked, the more bemused José looked, until his face became rigid and I noticed that his eyes had glazed over. When I finally stopped, I could see that he felt he ought to say something.

'This game - what do you call it, cricket - it is important then in your country?' he said.

It was no good. How could he possibly understand?

The most remarkable broadcast we heard was when the programming was interrupted to go to the *Cortes* - the lower house of the Spanish Parliament. We listened to chaos - a confusion of automatic weapons being fired and of shouted orders at the members of parliament. We were hearing Lieutenant-Colonel Antonio Tejero Molina's attempted right-wing military coup. In Madrid 350 members of parliament were held hostage for nearly 24 hours, the national radio station was seized by the military, and tanks came out on to the streets in Madrid and Barcelona. Sanity was not restored until King Juan Carlos appeared on television. He was solid and calm. He ordered the military to return to their barracks and they obeyed. Tejero was arrested and an uncertain peace prevailed, but for how long would it last? Should we prepare to be evacuated by a British gunboat, like Laurie Lee forty-five years before? I pictured the boat already having set off from Gibraltar, bristling with armoury, pulling in to every bay, a white-uniformed officer addressing the beach through a loudhailer, calling for British citizens to come aboard while there was still time. We were tempted to make an orderly retreat to Castell beach, carrying only our passports and driver's licences, but instead, we went to see Francisco *Alcalde*. We drove down the *rambla* to La Venta and the locals we passed waved and smiled as though nothing was happening. If a company of troops had marched up the *rambla* from Castell, they would have paid attention, but Madrid and Barcelona were too far away; what went on there was of no interest to them.

Francisco *Alcalde* was unconcerned. 'Now that *los militares* have left the streets it will be fine. Tejero does not have the support of enough generals. Too many of them were sitting back, waiting to see what would happen, and now that *el Rey*, Juan Carlos, has spoken it will be over. You will not see me cleaning my gun.'

Up until that moment no one had anything good to say about King Juan Carlos. He was considered to be a dullard - a slow-witted, humourless man who was merely a figurehead. But on that day, with the parliament held hostage, Spain had no other leader. His was the voice of the new democratic Spain and, without his power and authority, it was likely that the other generals would have supported the coup, and Spain would again have been ruled by a military dictatorship.

One of the upstairs rooms in the section we were renovating was filled to the ceiling with straw. It hadn't been there when we bought the *cortijo*, and we assumed it belonged to José. However, when we asked him if he would move it because we wanted to work in the room, he said it was nothing to do with him.

'Well,' Linda said, 'somebody must own it. We'll just have to ask around until we find out whose it is.'

We started at Los Morales and asked Bernardo and Carmela, who denied any knowledge of the straw. We spoke to Adela and Fra'quito, who shrugged and shook their heads, but there was something in their expressions we could not fathom. Afterwards, we asked at La Venta, but no one knew anything about it. It was very peculiar. We waited a few days and, when nobody came forward to claim the straw, I decided to remove it. Using a garden fork I tossed it into a barrow, which I wheeled down the path and emptied in the field while Adela watched me from her balcony. It was hot inside the room and as I worked I was enveloped in a cloud of dust, with pieces of straw sticking my hair and clothing. After three hours, I'd hardly made an impression and I'd had enough. Scratching and coughing, I went to find Linda.

'That's it. I give up. It's going to have to stay there.'

Linda laughed at my appearance. 'Dad warned me you were a man of straw.'

'Hah hah. Well, he was right. I'm giving up and I'm going for a swim to wash this stuff off.'

Two hours later, we returned to the house and saw

a line of mules, led by Fra'quito's son, Pepe, plodding down the front path. On the back of each mule was a pair of woven reed panniers stuffed full of straw. I went to the back of our house and found the door open - Fra'quito and his eldest son, Antonio the *mulero,* were inside, filling panniers. The back door fitted so badly that they had been able to poke a length of wire through and operate the bolt. I reacted badly.

'You've broken into our house. You didn't have our permission. I asked you if the straw was yours and you lied. You thought that you could leave it here until you needed it. It was only when I started to throw it out that you were forced to come over and get it.'

I had spoken in a mixture of Spanish and English but my meaning was obvious. I threw up my hands. Antonio ignored me and carried on filling a pannier with armfuls of straw. Fra'quito watched me without speaking and when he saw that I'd finished he turned away and helped his son. That evening I was remorseful.

'What have I done? I should have been grateful they saved me the job of clearing out the straw. Now, I've made an enemy of our neighbours and they won't speak to *me* for the next forty years.'

'They were in the wrong. All they had to do was admit the straw was theirs and take it away. You had no choice; you had to stand up for our rights.'

Two days later, Linda woke up with more than thirty small bites on her legs. By mid-morning they had become large red blotches and were on fire. Strangely, I had none.

'It must be something in the straw that's taken a liking to your tender English flesh,' I said, as I dabbed on calamine lotion.

We stripped the bed and found nothing but, as a precaution, I walked to the deposit and released some water and we washed the sheets and pillowcases in the irrigation channel. We hung the blankets on the line and beat them with our tennis rackets as Fra'quito and Adela watched from their balcony. The next morning Linda had no more bites and we thought that we'd cured the problem, but the following day she woke up with bites all over her body. Once more we stripped the bed and left the sheets and pillowcases to soak in disinfectant. Washing ourselves properly was difficult without running water and Linda stood on an old towel in the middle of the kitchen as I sponged her down from a bucket of warm water mixed with antiseptic. In different circumstances it would have been fun.

The calamine was not working and the bites were driving Linda mad. We went down the *rambla* to ask José for advice. 'Those bites are from *pulgas*,' he said.

We looked it up. 'Fleas,' said Linda. 'Well, if our house is infested with fleas, why isn't Barry being bitten?'

'That is obvious. Everyone knows there are two types of blood. You have sweet blood and your husband has sour blood.'

'That doesn't come as a surprise.'

'And if you are together in the same bed, the *pulgas* will only bite you.'

José told us to go to the general store in Castell where we could buy something to kill the fleas. The lady there listened while we explained the problem and tutted over Linda's bites. 'What you must do is bomb the house,' she said. We looked at each other; it could not possibly be *that* serious. 'You close all the doors and windows, ignite the bomb, and three hours later the *pulgas* are dead and it is safe to go back inside.'

She fetched the bomb. It was a yellow metal canister with a short wick poking out of the top. Its main constituent was sulphur. We drove back to Los Sanchez and removed all the food from the kitchen before I placed the bomb on the floor of our bedroom, lit the fuse, and ran for the front door. We stood together outside and watched as yellowy-brown smoke seeped out from around the doors and shutters.

We had a picnic in the *campo* and spent the afternoon in the *rambla* collecting flat stones and rocks. After the three hours had elapsed, I took a deep breath, wrapped my shirt around my face and stumbled about inside, opening doors and windows. Within half an hour the smoke had dispersed, leaving behind a brown residue on every surface, like atomic fallout.

'Surely the fleas couldn't live through that.'

Linda ran her finger across the kitchen table. 'It will be a miracle if we do.'

For two days we thought we had eradicated the fleas, but on the third night they returned and Linda was utterly miserable. Nothing was going right. Our struggles with the multiple layers of bureaucracy to ratify our residency, obtain the title deeds for the *cortijo*, register our ownership with the land tax authority and, vitally, have electricity connected, were time-consuming, mentally draining, and all appeared to have stalled. The more documents we produced, the more they asked for and, each time, it involved a visit to a *notario* to have the documents authenticated before we submitted them to the relevant authority. We made countless trips to different government agencies, sometimes to villages high into the mountains, where an unsmiling official would apply a colourful stamp to our documents before sending us off somewhere else for the process to be repeated. It was incredibly frustrating, but our minds were still set to English clocks and these were our first encounters with the *mañana* philosophy and leaden pace of Spain's bureaucracy. Our bodies ached from the hard, physical labour of working on the house from first light to dusk, which left us permanently exhausted. We prepared our evening meals in the gloom of candles and hurricane lamps and straight afterwards collapsed into bed. We had fallen out with our neighbours and now Linda was suffering from an invisible enemy that made nocturnal assaults on her body, and our mornings were spent treating her bites and washing bedding and clothing.

We finished hanging the washing on the line and Linda said, 'I don't want to do this any more.'

'Come on,' I said, 'we can't give up yet. We've only just arrived.'

'It's all right for you; you're not getting bitten.'

'Look, we're working too hard. This is supposed to be fun. Let's take the van down the coast for a few days. By the time we get back the fleas will have died of starvation.'

We packed some food, threw sleeping bags and clothing into the van and set off. It was October and the tourists had left. We drove inland from Almuñécar and slept and cooked in the van, walked in the hills, and in the middle of the day drove down to the beach and swam in the cooling water of the Mediterranean. Linda's bites stopped itching and healed, the sun shone, and the fleas were temporarily forgotten. On the fifth day, we sat on the scruffy, grey beach at Almuñécar and watched a man, no taller than a ten-year-old boy, make slow progress towards us. He detoured to pick up pieces of driftwood, which he tied together in a bundle that he dangled from his hand. As he came closer, we saw that he had an unlit cigarette in his mouth, several days' growth of beard, and a canvas bag slung over one shoulder. A brown dog, small and bony, followed a few paces behind him. When he was almost level with us he stopped and, with his hands, scooped out a hollow in the sand and carefully arranged the driftwood. He lit it with a match, which he then transferred to his cigarette. The match burnt his fingers and he dropped it to the sand. *'Mierda!'*

A breeze fanned his fire and carried a plume of white smoke along the beach parallel with the water. From his bag he pulled out two thin loaves of bread, several handfuls of sardines wrapped in newspaper, and a Pepsi bottle that was three-quarters full of a pale liquid. He had picked up short lengths of bamboo cane from the beach and, with his pocket knife, he split them down the centre and sharpened the ends to a point. He threaded three sardines widthways onto each cane and planted them in the sand, downwind from the fire. The dog sat five yards away watching the sardines cook.

He had known we were looking, and he turned

suddenly and called out, 'Come over here; it's time to eat.'

The van was parked more than a mile away. All our provisions were inside. We walked over to his fire and told him we had no food with us.

'I didn't think you had. I was inviting you to share my *comida*.'

Linda looked in her bag and took out a lemon that we had brought along to squeeze into our water bottles, 'The only thing we have is this lemon.'

He beamed. *'Perfecto!* That is just what I needed. My sardines would have been nothing without your lemon.'

We sat with him on the sand and shared his *comida*. The sardines were the freshest I have ever tasted and the smoke made them fabulous. He passed me the Pepsi bottle and I drank his thin wine. He told us his name was Miguel and he helped the fisherman, who paid him with fish and a few pesetas. That morning the catch had been good and he had more than he could eat. He threw the heads and the bones to the dog and laughed. 'So, today the *perro* and I, we eat better than kings.'

We laughed with him. 'What is your dog's name?'

'The *perro* is no one's. If you feed him, he will be yours.'

We talked for an hour. Even though it was only forty minutes drive away, he had not heard of Castell and had no idea where our *cortijo* was. When we left, he dismissed our thanks. To him it was simple; if he had something, he would share it, and he would expect anyone else to do the same. He wished us good health and lots of children and, if we passed this way again, to look out for him. We walked along the beach in the direction of the van and the dog followed us for a short distance before it decided it was better off with Miguel and went back.

'You know,' Linda said, 'we can't let those fleas beat us. Let's ask someone else.'

On the drive home we stopped at a pharmacy and the man there explained that we had not broken the life cycle of the fleas. All we had done was kill the fleas, but not their eggs, which hatched out and perpetuated the problem. He told us to go to a general store and buy Green Cross powder, and sprinkle it in the bed and on all the floors. After a week we could sweep it up and we would have no more problems. We did what he said and Linda was not bitten again. In later years Green Cross disappeared from the shops and I am convinced we had powdered our bed with DDT.

When the runner beans began fruiting, José came every second day to pick them. He filled two or three hessian sacks that at the end of the day Paco, Mari-Carmen's fiancé, heaved up on to the back of his truck and took away to the *cooperativo* to be sold. Each time he came, José called at the house and gave us a carrier bag full of beans. The Spanish *habichuelas* are different to English runner beans. They are broader, fleshier and sweeter. Freshly picked, they tasted exquisite and for two weeks we ate them twice a day - steamed, boiled, roasted, fried or raw. After that we had them once a day, and then every other day. They began to mount up, and we took them with us whenever we went into Castell and offered them to strangers. Eventually, we could eat them only in curries or stews, and on one occasion, in total despair, we tried them with custard. Finally, the crop was finished.

'I know we have to eat what's in season, but for the rest of my life I will not eat another runner bean,' I said.

'It's all right,' said Linda, 'now that José's pulling them up, we'll be able to plant lots and lots of *different* vegetables.'

We hadn't spoken to José about the agreement we had made when we purchased Los Sanchez but, now that we were in residence, the arrangement clearly had to change. José, however, appeared to be unaware that we might want to make use of our land and talked about planting another crop of beans in the spring. He owned no land, although a widow, La Marina, allowed him to use a small piece of her land as a vegetable garden, in return for pruning her trees. He was using our *campo* for crops to sell at the *cooperativo* and I was not looking forward to telling him that his income from this would shortly stop.

The matter was resolved several days later. José had developed a habit of bringing his radio into the field and tuning to a station that played flamenco music. He didn't move the radio around with him; instead he placed it in the shade of a tree close to the house and turned it on full volume. For most of the time we were working inside the house and it was only a minor irritation, but if we were outside it soon became unbearable. One morning, we were forced to listen to guitars, castanets, clapping hands and stamping feet for about two hours, while José was thirty yards from his radio pulling out the canes that had supported his beans. Finally, I'd had enough, but when I went into the field to ask him to turn it down he wasn't there. I looked down the *rambla* and saw him walking in the direction of his house, carrying a large bundle of canes over his shoulder. He had considerately left his music on for us to enjoy. The round trip would give us at least half-an-hour respite, so I switched off the radio and thought nothing more about it. When José returned he was angry; he accused us of us of not liking his music and interfering with his property *sin permiso*. He stayed and finished pulling out the canes, but he wouldn't talk to us.

The next day, I went to see Francisco *Alcalde* and told him what had happened. He shrugged. 'Personally, I like flamenco music, but in my own house, in the evening, and with a glass of wine. José has brought his music into your *campo* without asking if you want to hear it. You had the right to turn it off, especially if he was not there listening to it. And now you must tell him you need your *campo* to grow your own crops. José has used your land and made money from it. You owe him nothing.'

He was right, but I liked José; he was a good friend. I did not want to be on bad terms with him and I told Francisco that I was sorry for what had occurred. Two days later I heard José's cough and he materialised from the shade of the olive tree. He behaved as though nothing had happened and gave me a bag of tomatoes and onions from his vegetable garden. We sat on the wall and he smoked a cigarette while he explained that he had been asked by the widow, La Marina, to work her *campo* on the opposite side of the *barranco*. She badly needed his assistance with this and he regretted that he would no longer be able to help us with our land.

I thanked José for looking after our *campo* so well and for being such a good friend, and I said that I was sorry I had touched his radio. He smiled and we shook hands. I never did learn if Francisco *Alcalde* had spoken to him or if he had simply come to realise the inevitable.

The second time we fell out with our neighbour, Fra'quito, was over the use of our land. The surrounding hillsides were covered with almond trees, but we had none growing in our field and we decided to plant some along the border with Fra'quito's field. José gave me several small trees and told me that, by law, I must plant them at least one metre inside our boundary. I took a tape measure into the field, dug an impressive row of holes about one and a half metres from the boundary line and planted the saplings. Two days later, I saw that Fra'quito had tethered his goats in his field. They were very close to the section where I had planted the almonds and I went down to look. Each of the saplings had been eaten entirely to the ground. But for the newly turned over soil, it would have been easy to believe that they had never existed.

Fra'quito was sitting in the shade of a loquat tree watching me, his face impassive. I had learnt from the straw incident and this time I spoke calmly. 'Your goats have come into my *campo* and eaten my almond trees.'

He didn't get up. 'Your chickens come into my *campo.*'

'But they don't do any damage.'

He spat gently onto the earth. It was far enough away from my feet not to be an insult. 'If the *almendros* had grown bigger, the roots would have come into my *campo* and taken the goodness.'

I could have pointed out to him that I was within my rights to plant the trees there, that several of his trees were close to the boundary and their roots undoubtedly encroached on to our land, but it was now immaterial - the issue was over. He had solved the problem his way, with action that allowed no argument. I turned away and walked slowly back to the house.

More than eighteen months later, I saw a dog kill one of Fra'quito and Adela's chickens in front of their house. There was a flurry of feathers and squawks and Adela ran out of her kitchen, screeching. She threw a saucepan full of beans, missed the dog, and it loped away with the chicken in its mouth. I recognised the dog; it belonged to Miguel and Isobel and lived at their *cortijo*, Juanico, high on the Rubité road. Three months before, they had moved to an apartment in Castell where they could not keep the dog, and they returned to their farmhouse once or twice a fortnight to feed it. One evening it had appeared at the edge of our terrace, its ribs showing through its coat. It wouldn't let us come close and we put down a bowl of scraps. It watched us, with its stomach heaving and saliva running from its mouth, until we moved away, before it crept up to the bowl and devoured the food in huge gulps.

A week after it killed our neighbours' chicken, the dog returned. I saw it leave the Rubité road on the path that loops around to the back of Los Morales. Fra'quito and Adela were on their balcony and I called across to them, but they had already seen it. Fra'quito was unhurried; he went into the house and returned with his shotgun. For several seconds, he stood motionless at the balcony rail with the gun at his shoulder, before he fired a single shot and straightaway turned and went back inside. Miguel and Isobel may have wondered what happened to their dog, but they never mentioned it to us. We were learning that there was an unwritten code in the community - and its enforcement had no need of the *guardia civil*.

CHAPTER NINE

Motril was our closest town, 27 kilometres away. From Los Sanchez, it took us forty minutes to bump and rattle down the *rambla* in a cloud of grey dust, and then negotiate the hairpin bends on the coast road. For the first few months, we went there every week to buy materials for our *obras*. We had imagined that there would be a large hardware store, something like B&Q, and all we would have to do is whiz round the aisles with a couple of trolleys and pull things off shelves. The reality was entirely different. We discovered that, for almost every item we needed, there was a separate, small shop hidden away in an unfashionable part of town. Just finding them was a challenge.

Benny had told us that it took him longer to locate and purchase the materials for his own renovations than to actually do the work. 'But you'll *comprar* a lot of the *cosas* from Antonio at the ferret store,' he said. 'If he hasn't got it, just say *bueno* and split, or you'll be there *hablaring* all day.'

'Ferret store?' said Linda.

'The *ferreteria*,' said Benny.

'Split?' I said.

102

'Yeah, go, you know, leave.'

'Of course ... I should have got that.'

Benny had a language all of his own. After living in Spain for six months, his speech had evolved into a form of Tex-Mex, a jumbled mess of North American colloquialisms and schoolboy Spanish. Some days we had as much trouble understanding him as we did the locals.

The *ferreteria* turned out to be an old-fashioned iron mongers that sold all things metal, from screws and nails to bricklaying trowels and wheelbarrows, but it did not sell electrical or plumbing fittings, nor did it sell plaster and cement, timber and paint, floor and wall tiles, irrigation piping and many other things we needed, all of which were sold somewhere in the backstreets. No stock was ever displayed at these places. There was a wooden counter with the owner's wife behind it and somewhere out the back were the things that we wanted to buy, but couldn't point at. There was always a queue and nobody was in a hurry. In Andalucía, shopping was a social experience to be lingered over and enjoyed - not rushed. Every customer knew the owner's wife personally, but they hadn't seen each other for quite some while, so it was compulsory to enquire about spouses, sons and daughters, grandparents and grandchildren, cousins and then distant relations, until finally they had exhausted every known living relative, and even some who had recently died. Then, with a regretful, '*Bueno*,' they would buy three plastic washers. As they turned to leave, they would give us a wonderful smile, as if to say, 'Now it's your turn to have a good old gossip.'

103

Our visits to Motril were laced with frustration and failure. This was due in part to our limited Spanish - even though we carried around with us a huge dictionary - however, the main problem was lack of time. The shops in Motril open at nine, shut promptly at midday, and do not reopen until four. The siesta is a delightful custom that conjures up pictures of lounging in a hammock suspended between olive trees while sipping chilled sangria, but it also meant that we had only a frantic three hour period in the morning to shop. However manically we approached this task, we never came close to buying everything on our list. We then had a choice either to spend four hours in Motril's bars until the shops reopened or else beat a cowardly retreat home, knowing that on our next visit we would have an even longer list. But Linda knew that, if I spent four hours in the local bars, there was no likelihood that I would do *anything* until at least lunchtime the following day, let alone tussle with Motril's shopkeepers, so we drove home.

We had tried splitting up, but we worked well as a team. I knew exactly what materials we needed for the *obras* and I was reasonably competent at asking for them, but the problem was, I could never understand the shopkeeper's reply. To me, it was always one unbroken word of about 200 syllables. Linda somehow managed to separate the sounds and translated. Then I would respond. Other customers would offer advice and tell the shopkeeper what they thought we wanted. The dictionary would be thumbed through; items would be brought out from the back and returned; and it would carry on like that until we were finally shown what we came in for or we were sent somewhere else. I am positive that the shopkeepers of Motril looked forward to our visits as much as we dreaded them.

My mother had remarried the previous year and was living in Tripoli with her husband, who was a pilot for Libyan Arab Airlines. We had been in Spain for two months when she decided to pay us a visit to see for herself what level of squalor I was subjecting Linda to. It was a typically spur-of-the-moment decision. She caught a plane to England, booked a charter flight to Malaga, and then sent us a telegram announcing that she would be arriving at Castell plaza, on the Almeria coach, in three days time. The closest telephone line to Los Sanchez was three kilometres away and letters took more than a week to reach us. The post office in England had assured my mother that a telegram was the fastest way to communicate and guaranteed that it would be delivered within thirty-six hours.

I had stopped shaving soon after we arrived in Spain and for the only time in my life sported a luxuriant, dark-brown beard that made me look like a young Fidel Castro. On the day that my mother came to visit, Linda and I drove to Motril with a larger than usual list of materials to buy. In the late morning, as I was dodging traffic in the main street, I heard hammering coming from a passing coach. I thought nothing of it and rushed off to meet Linda at the bank. It was another frustrating morning and we accomplished only half of what we had set out to do. At midday, we found ourselves in front of a *bodega* deep in the backstreets. We stepped down out of the sunshine into grey light. The *bodega* was empty apart from an unshaven man who was washing out bottles in a concrete sink behind the bar. Wooden barrels lined the yellowing, whitewashed walls. There were no tables or chairs and we crunched across a concrete floor strewn with peanut shells.

Expressionless, he watched our approach. *'Qué?'*

'Hola. Dos finos, por favor.'

He wiped his hands on a rag and took two stubby and still-wet glasses from alongside the sink and filled them from an unlabelled bottle. He banged them in front of us and poured peanuts into a bowl, which he slid towards us across the marble. He went back to washing bottles.

The dryness of the fino stole the moisture from our mouths. We drank the first glass fast and the wild look left our eyes. We lingered over the second and were able to laugh at the morning's events that, twenty minutes before, had us snarling at each other. We ate the peanuts. There was nowhere to put the shells and we placed them in a neat pile on the bar. When we asked to pay, the man frowned at the shells and, with a forearm the size of the *serrano* hams hanging from the ceiling, he swept them onto the floor behind us. In those early days we were overly-polite, overly-cautious not to offend. We need not have bothered; the Spanish were forgiving and careless of manners.

Revived by the fino, we decided, for the first time, to stay in Motril for the siesta, but keep out of the bars and instead explore the port area. We would do battle again when the shops reopened at four. When we eventually left Motril, the van was laden and the sun was setting. By the time we turned up the *rambla* at Castell it was dark and cold. During the day, the tracks that criss-cross the *rambla* are benign, but at night, in a car's headlights, they develop a sameness to lure the unwary to deserted *fincas,* far into the hills. On one memorable occasion, visitors left our house after an evening of revelry and, soon afterwards, found themselves on a winding track that was barely the width of their car. They got out and discovered that they were climbing a mountain, with a sheer rock face on one side and a drop into the darkness on the other. It was too dangerous to reverse and the track was not wide enough to turn around. They had no option; they had to keep going. As they went higher, the track became rougher, with the outer edge eroded and crumbling. Finally, they made the decision to sleep in the car and tackle it in the morning.

That evening, on the way back from Motril, we made one wrong turn that landed us in an olive grove, and by the time we retraced our steps and reached Los Sanchez it was nearly seven o'clock. There were two suitcases on the front step and a note from my mother pinned to the door saying that she was with Fra'quito and Adela, at Los Morales. Relations with our neighbours had been strained since the straw and goat episodes and I was unsure of the reception we would receive when we went over.

When we arrived they were having their best evening for years. My mother was holding court in the centre of the room. She was clutching a tumbler of red wine in one hand and waving the other around. The high colour on her cheeks was not rouge. In fractured

Italian, she was telling them about life in Libya and matching her words with pantomimes. Adela, Fra'quito and their children, Little Adela and Miguelito, were watching her, open-mouthed.

She broke off when she saw us. 'Why didn't you meet me?'

'Well, this is a lovely surprise, Mother, and if you'd let us know you were coming we *would* have. By the way, do you realise these people don't understand a word you're saying? They can't understand people from other parts of Spain, let alone your appalling Italian.'

'Don't be absurd, Barry. They're both Latin-based languages. Anyway, I sent you a telegram.'

I gave her a hug. 'Well, it never arrived. Come on; let's go before we outstay our welcome. We are barely on speaking terms with our neighbours. I'll tell you about it later.'

We celebrated my mother's arrival with a bottle of *rioja* that we had been saving for a special occasion. 'I *saw* you in Motril, Barry, from the coach. You were crossing the road, but at first I wasn't sure it was you.'

'It's a bit sad when you don't recognise your own son.'

'It was because of that horrible beard, but when I was positive I banged on the window, but you didn't look up. I was going to stop the coach and get off, but I daren't in case I couldn't find you. Then I'd have been stuck in that town.'

She had got off the coach in Castell and waited for an hour and a half in the plaza before she realised that we weren't coming to meet her. She paid someone to drive her to Los Sanchez and waited at the house. She had decided that if we didn't come home she would sleep in the *corral* with the chickens. When it was nearly dark, Adela and her daughter came over from Los Morales. Despite our recent differences, with typical Andalucían hospitality, they invited my mother back to their house, cooked her eggs and potatoes, and told her she could stay the night.

Three days later at 11 am, Antonio the postman arrived on a mule. He had ridden twelve kilometres on the corkscrewing, earth road from Rubité, the mountain village that was our administrative centre.

'I have a telegram,' Antonio said from his mule. He passed it down to me.

'It is from my mother, Antonio. She says that she is coming to visit us.'

He beamed. 'That is good. When is she coming?'

'Antonio, *this* is my mother.'

He took off his cap and scratched his head. 'But why would your mother send you a telegram if she is already here?'

Antonio accepted a large glass of cognac while we debated the strangeness of the situation. On his second cognac, he admitted that the telegram had languished at Rubité post office for several days. He had seen no reason to make the long trip to Los Sanchez for a solitary telegram and had waited until he had other calls in the area. We were his final visit. Our normal mail was brought down daily from Rubité with the bread delivery, but, because the telegram needed our signature, it had demanded a special trip by Antonio. He finished the cognac and, with difficulty, remounted his mule. Swaying in the saddle, he walked it at a sedate pace back up the Rubité road.

My mother was scandalised. 'Nowhere else in Europe, Barry, would they hold on to a telegram for days and then deliver it by mule. You've brought Linda to a very primitive place.'

Having rescued my mother from the potential fate of spending a night in the *corral,* and in return having been richly entertained, Adela and Fra'quito took a proprietary interest in her. Adela and her daughter came over with a plate of biscuits they had made and sat in the kitchen with my mother for more than an hour, chatting and laughing and no doubt being treated to some more execrable Italian. Fra'quito, who had always struck me as one of the surliest and most unfriendly people I had ever met, became positively charming when my mother was around. His face was wreathed in smiles; he couldn't stop talking; and, to my astonishment, he was chivalrous. My mother loved walking and went off exploring on her own along the mule paths. Fra'quito had seen her setting off and he warned her about the dangers of walking late in the afternoon in the hills, where it was easy to get lost and quickly became cold, and to take great care on the slopes and the rocky paths. If you were not used to them you could fall and break a leg, and you might lie in a gully for days until someone found you. There were snakes everywhere and to be bitten when you were on your own ... He pursed his lips, sucked air in noisily and shook his head, as he contemplated all the disasters that could occur to my mother. Even here in the *barranco* there were hazards; he gestured at the rough surface and kicked a stone out of the way. At that point

I expected him to lay his jacket out on the ground, doff his cap, and offer my mother a steadying arm - and I was disappointed when he didn't.

Fra'quito and Adela had spread the news of my mother's visit and people came to the house especially to meet her. She was treated like a celebrity during the ten days she stayed with us. The Spanish love their families and, having met my mother, they now looked at us differently. We were no longer two people who had arrived in their valley from nowhere. My mother had given us another dimension, had made us more like them and, following her stay, our relationship with Fra'quito and Adela improved dramatically.

Rubité was an unlikely regional centre. It was far smaller than Castell and accessed by roads that were impassable after heavy rain. In addition to the post office, it boasted a town hall which held the land-tax records, a general store, two bars, a church, and Gonzales and Son's bakery. On the occasions we went to Rubité to attend to bureaucratic chores, we called at the bakery. The bread-making equipment was on full display, a conveyor-belt production line that stretched the length of the shop. Chains rattled, wheels turned and cogs came together. Mechanical arms, with paddles and whisks, descended with precision into metal bowls and stirred, kneaded and shaped until, at the end, trays of formed dough were slid by Gonzales senior into the cavernous, wood-fired oven. The Victorian machinery was irresistible to me. I was a child again with my mother in a Croydon department store, standing in front of a row of glass cabinets. When you put a penny in the slot, the scenes inside came to life. Eyes blinked awake and heads turned. Men and women, cars and trains made jerky progress around the cabinets.

Gonzales senior recognised us as the *extranjeros* from Los Sanchez. 'Come up to the capital to see the sights, have you ... to take in the attractions?'

We laughed. 'Just to pay our taxes.'

Gonzales' bread making was erratic. Some days the round, flat *rodondos* were so hard that we had to soak them in water before we could eat them and we could have used them instead of the stones from the *rambla* to rebuild the front wall of our house. Occasionally, he produced a loaf that was exquisite and we wondered what had happened on these rare days when everything came together to create perfection. Gonzales senior was the baker and he got up at three-thirty every morning to light the oven and start making the dough. His son, Gonzo, spent his days traipsing around the mountains in an old van, delivering his father's bread to the *cortijos* and hamlets. We were one of his first customers on the long journey and the bread was still hot when he arrived. Sometimes, Gonzo went on mysterious trips to Granada and on these days Gonzales senior would deliver the bread. Invariably, there were one or two passengers from Rubité in the cab, ancient, shrunken ladies dressed in black, who sat mute when the van stopped. They were dropped off in Castell and collected on the way home at the end of the day.

One day, Gonzo turned up in a brand new 4x4 van and he started his triumphant tooting a kilometre up the Rubité road. The sound was strong and vibrant, nothing like the tired wheeze of the old van. His new van was not yet coated with the dust from the *rambla* and its chrome bumpers and cream paintwork gleamed in the sun. Inside, the racks of bread could not mask the smell of the new vinyl. It made our elderly Bedford van look very shabby and we took to parking it, half-hidden, in the shade of the trees lining the *barranco*, where it lurked like a down-at-heel relative no one would admit to.

Gonzo never applied the handbrake when he stopped to sell his bread. Instead, he slowed the van to walking pace, selected either first or second gear, switched off the engine and stepped out of the cab. He stood motionless while the van juddered along for a few paces until it came to rest with the back doors exactly level with the stationary Gonzo. Then, he would take one step forward and, with a flourish, he would fling open the doors. Every time he did it I had to stop myself from clapping. It was a trick that required consummate skill. In addition to the gradient, factors such as the roughness of the surface; whether the van was fully or partially laden; if there were passengers on board; together with the wind speed and whether the ground was wet or dry, all had to be taken into account. I only once saw him carry out the manoeuvre imperfectly and he looked sulky. Gonzo was solidly built, with oiled hair. He dressed snappily, in contrast to the rags of his customers. He was a young man who had plans. He was going to travel to South America and become rich. He was not going to spend his life selling bread in this backwater. He was impatient for your money. If you were slow to sort the coins he would rub his thumb and index finger together rapidly, like Shylock in a hurry.

Several months later, Gonzales senior did the delivery run. He was at Juanico, the home of Miguel and Isobel, his third stop from Rubité, where the road is steep and has a series of horseshoe bends. As Isobel stood outside her house, Gonzales senior slowed the van to walking pace, turned off the motor and stepped from the cab. The van stuttered forward, but, instead of stopping, it gained speed. Gonzales tried to catch it, but all he and Isobel could do was watch it topple over the edge and turn somersaults for two hundred yards, scattering loaves. News of the disaster spread and shepherds walked their flocks to the site. For days, sheep dotted the mountain, picking over Gonzales' bread.

For three days we had no bread or mail deliveries, but on the fourth day Gonzo arrived in the old van. We offered our condolences over the loss of the new van.

He shrugged. 'At least he had no passengers and we didn't sell the old van. He thinks he put it in third gear and not first. *Mi padre...*' He stopped, as though he was unable to express in words what he felt, but I suspect that three days before he had tried. We walked back to the house past the Bedford van. You know, it really wasn't so bad.

It was a week before we saw Gonzales senior. He looked despondent and we noticed that he applied the handbrake when he stopped. Adela came over from Los Morales. She had no words of sympathy and she scrutinised her *rodondo* before sniffing and poking it.

'I hope this is not from the mountain,' she said.

CHAPTER TEN

We were making progress to have power installed. The electricity company in Motril had finally approved our application and sent us an official document adorned with seals and extravagant signatures. Armed with this, we paid a visit to Juan *la Luz* - John the Light - the electrical contractor in Castell. Juan was busy. He was in the middle of a major contract. He glanced at our plan, wrote some figures in his notebook and gave us a vague estimate for the cost of the installation. Juan was equally vague about when he might be able to do the work. Even so, we were optimistic that before too long we would be able to use the electric pump to fill the tanks and we would have running water in the house. It was time to start planning the bathroom.

The bars still had primitive, hole-in-the-ground, footsteps toilets, where you hurried through the procedure in an undignified squat, praying that nothing fell out of your pockets. These toilets had old fashioned, chain-pull cisterns that were mounted at ceiling level and produced a gusher of water at high pressure - something that the Spanish rarely achieved with their taps. As a result, if you continued to stand in the cubicle after pulling the chain, you were soaked to mid-calf. You soon learnt that the art of flushing these toilets was to open the door, firmly grasp the chain and extend it to its limit - if possible so that you were actually outside the cubicle - take a deep breath, yank the chain, jump six inches in the air and run - with a torrent of water in pursuit. It was easy to spot the untrained toilet users; they returned to the bar looking embarrassed, trailing water.

None of the local houses had toilets, but there were never any of the smells that we would have expected from their absence and we were curious. Perhaps they had discovered a revolutionary sanitary device that dealt with the issue, and would save me from installing a flushing toilet and septic system. It was a delicate subject to discuss, but one day, during a pause in a conversation with José, I raised it. By that time José believed, like the scaffolders in Bristol, that I needed a large slice of help to get through life and didn't appear to find the question strange, although he may have wondered how we had coped to that point.

José started to explain, thought better of it, and said he would show me. He led me a short distance up the hillside, directly behind Los Sanchez, where there was a large patch of *chumbas* - a variety of prickly-pear cactus that grows to more than twelve feet high. It was the ideal spot for the water tanks and I had previously cleared a small space, at great physical cost. The spikes on the large leaves are the size of hypodermic needles and had given me serious wounds. The fruit and smaller leaves have hair-like prickles that had entered my skin and festered for days. I had noticed that all the houses had similar cactus patches and I assumed the owners left them because they were too fearsome to remove.

'The *chumbas*,' José said, 'are the toilet.'

It did not seem possible. I had learnt that this was an area to be avoided at all costs, not to go to voluntarily and expose sensitive parts of the body. There was no way Linda would see this as a viable alternative to a flushing toilet and I had no desire to receive a detailed description from José of the precise technical manner in which the cactus patch operated.

'Just the job,' I said, 'and they seem to be in perfect working order, unless I'm very much mistaken.'

José nodded. 'People also use the mule stable,' he added and offered no further explanation.

'We don't have a mule.'

'Then you use the *chumbas*.'

Later, I spoke to Linda about my scatological discussion with José. 'The *chumbas* are definitely not a place to sit quietly for ten minutes to read the paper, but there must be a good reason why everyone's chosen a cactus patch for their loo. It can't only be for privacy, when they could just as easily have a clump of oleanders or broom. I bet you, in fifty years time, scientists will discover that *chumbas* secrete enzymes that clean up all the waste overnight.'

'And I bet you it will be the women, first thing in the morning,' said Linda. 'Anyway, that's it, no other options?'

'Well, José said people have some type of arrangement in the mule stable, probably something like our chemical toilet, which has to be emptied.'

A week later, Linda had her first and only experience with the mule-stable toilet, when we visited Francisco *Alcalde* and Madelena at La Venta. We had stopped for a chat late one afternoon on the way back from Castell and they invited us in for a glass of wine. We stayed longer than we had intended and it was after dark when, without thinking, Linda asked if she could use their toilet. Francisco and Madelena exchanged a glance before Madelena got up and took Linda outside to the mule stable at the back of the house. Madelena told her to use the area to the left of the door, where the straw was fresh, and to close the door. There was no light inside and Linda squatted on the rough straw in complete darkness. After a few seconds she heard a shuffling from the far side of the stable. Up until that moment she had assumed that the stable would be empty. Mules are very large animals. They are bred to plough rocky mountain slopes and are immensely strong. A kick from a mule could be fatal and if one just leant against you it would break a few ribs. Linda nearly passed out with fear and then reasoned that the mule must be tethered, but anyway she decided to get out in a hurry. It was difficult to be certain, but the shuffling appeared to be getting closer and Linda's panic returned. She started to get to her feet when, without warning, the mule expelled air through its nostrils, with explosive force, directly into her face. We heard her scream and rushed to the back door.

She was ashen but composed. 'Will someone please go in there and fetch my handbag.'

Francisco told us that the mule had only come over to be friendly. It had expected to find Madelena and was surprised when it was someone else. Nonetheless, the incident speeded up the construction of our bathroom and toilet. I had carried out some research into septic systems before we left England, but most that I had come across were highly complicated and on a scale more suitable for a small town than our farmhouse. Shortly before Benny went back to Canada, we spoke to him about it and he drew us a plan of a system that he intended installing. It was very simple and could be built either below or above ground. It consisted of a three-chambered, rectangular tank, of modest dimensions, constructed of brick, with an internal waterproof render. Benny spoke knowledgably about the different types of bacteria that broke down the effluent and he prodded his sketch with a thick finger as he showed us how the system worked.

'When you flush the toilet, the crap and piss and all that stuff shoots down this pipe into the first chamber - right?' We nodded. 'When it gets full, it goes through this second pipe that connects it to the next chamber and fills that one up - right?' We nodded again. 'These first two chambers are completely sealed so that no air gets in, and that means they contain only *anaerobic* bacteria, which live in there on a diet of shit and bog paper.'

'Right,' we said.

'When the second chamber is full, it goes through this other pipe into the last chamber, which is not airtight, and this is where the *aerobic* bacteria live.'

'They're the fit ones in leotards,' I explained to Linda.

'Right,' grinned Benny, 'and they chomp up

anything that the *anaerobic* bacteria have missed, and the water that comes out of this overflow pipe from the third chamber is crystal clear.'

'Can you drink it?' I said. 'Theoretically, that is.'

'Well, whether you can or you can't, we're not,' said Linda, 'theoretically or otherwise.' She made a bad joke about having come from affluence in England to effluent in Spain, and Benny left me his diagram, which became the blueprint for our septic system.

After weeks of prevarication, Juan *La Luz* finally gave us a firm date when he would come and install the electricity - or as firm a date as we would ever get. We had lived in the house for more than three months without power and it was now mid December. Juan regretted that it would not be possible to carry out the work before Christmas, but it would be done immediately afterwards - the following week or, at the very latest, the week after that. By this time, we had experienced Spanish punctuality and had learnt enough not to become excited. We had once waited all day in vain for a delivery of sand that we had ordered the evening before, and when it did arrive a week later the driver dumped it in the wrong place. We now knew that, if we were told simply *mañana*, there was no chance whatsoever it would happen. *Mañana* is an evasive word; it is used to get rid of people; it does not signify a commitment. Juan *La Luz* had been vague, but he hadn't said *mañana,* so there was a chance he would come. At least there was some encouragement to finish the bathroom, in readiness.

The septic tank proved to be unusually

straightforward to build. Normally, when I allow four days to do a job, it takes four weeks. Everything possible goes wrong and I seriously wish that I was back at my loss adjuster's desk. I am sure it was Benny's sketch - not to scale and without measurements, on a scrappy piece of paper torn from a notebook - that helped. His diagram fitted exactly with my type of building.

I converted a small room at the back of the house into the bathroom, which featured an exotic sunken bath. This was the last thing I had intended, but when I planned the bathroom I overlooked the fact that the room had the lowest ceiling in the house. At my first attempt, I seated the bath on bricks, stepped into it and promptly hit my head on a rafter. The shower rose was at the same level as my chin and it would have meant showering in a half crouch. So, I dismantled the bath and spent the next two days pickaxing the rock strata beneath, in order to sink the bath twelve inches. This is what I mean about jobs going badly. The only bathroom item we had brought out from England was the chipped beige bath and we selected the other fittings solely on the basis of cost. On one of our forays into Motril we had discovered an entry-level plumbing supplier that stocked only the cheapest and nastiest varieties of sanitary wares. All the stock was coated with dust and the shop was frequented by bar owners, tenement landlords, and people like us with little money. We couldn't match the beige bath, so we purchased a white washbasin, toilet, and wall-mounted, PVC cistern, of the type favoured by the bars. Inexplicably, the cistern came with a length of grey pipe to connect it to the toilet and it had a shiny gold chain which resembled fairground jewellery. The toilet seat was made of thin, flexible plastic that bent dangerously when you sat on it. I always feared that someone who possessed a posterior of certain dimensions would become wedged and have to be cut free, and I kept a pair of secateurs in the kitchen drawer, in readiness.

The instant gas water heater came with dire warnings about the consequences of inadequate ventilation. Being unsure whether the toxic vapours were heavier or lighter than air, I made openings at both ceiling and floor level, with the result that the room was exceptionally draughty and cold in winter. The rough-rendered walls around the bath were not straight enough to tile and, instead, I applied several coats of white gloss paint to waterproof them. I made the towel rail from a length of bamboo cane supported between two home-made wooden brackets and, finally, I painted the floor a cheerful post-office red. Even by my standards, the workmanship was appalling and the bathroom looked truly dreadful, but, to me, it was simply a miracle that everything I had put in worked, and I couldn't wait to show it off to our neighbours. Ours was the first home in the area to have hot water and a shower - and to actually have a proper toilet. Not a mule stable or a cactus patch, but a ball-valve controlled, automatic-filling, chain-pull-flushing, water-closet system – and, not only that, it went into an environmentally-friendly septic tank. I felt like Thomas Crapper of the *rambla*.

The word soon went out that the *extranjeros* had installed a bathroom and people travelled some

distance to look at it. Juan still hadn't come to install
the electricity, so, for demonstration purposes, I hauled
two beer barrels full of water, ten gallons at a time, up
the back path to the cactus patch and tipped them into
the tanks. At one stage I had three lots of people
queuing and I thought about charging admission.
Within six months, Fra'quito and Adela at Los Morales,
and Francisco *Alcalde* and Madalena at La Venta had
installed bathrooms. Having seen my bathroom, they
both, quite understandably, employed *albanils* to do
the work. They had ceramic tiles on the walls and
floors; cisterns that sat on top of the toilets; there was
masses of chrome, and matching towel rails and toilet-
roll holders. The two bathrooms looked very swish and
modern - about four-star hotel standard. Despite all
this, I felt that they weren't quite right - a certain
something was missing. Now, I might be on my own
here, but I believe it was because they lacked that
charming rusticity that so individualised my bathroom.

Juan *La Luz* arrived, without warning, at first light
during the second week in January. He drove up the
barranco sounding the horn of his truck, and shouted
unloading instructions at his two helpers as he strode
up the front path. Now that he was finally here things
were going to happen fast. Juan stood on the terrace
with his arms folded and scowled across at Los
Morales. He had to run two cables approximately 100
yards from the electricity pole outside Bernardo and
Carmela's house to our *cortijo* and, because of the span,
he had to erect another pole at the midway point. The
only obstacle was a majestic white cedar close to the

edge of the *barranco*.

After a short period of noisy activity at the truck, the other men joined us on the terrace. One was young and unsmiling and, as soon as he arrived, Juan fired instructions at him.

'Paco, unroll the cable. Take it up to the top of Los Morales. Go round that orange tree and don't tangle it in the olives. Clamp it to the bottom of the pole and then do the same with the other cable. Don't cross them over. *Vaya!*'

The other man, Pepe, was in his sixties. He was wearing a white panama hat set at a jaunty angle and he stood smiling at us. Juan and Paco had largely ignored us, but Pepe held out his hand.

'German?'

'English.'

He pointed to the screwdriver in Juan's hand. 'What is that called in English?'

'A screwdriver.'

'An escrewdriver.'

'No, a screwdriver.'

'That is what I said, an escrewdriver. In Spanish it is a *destornillador*.' He plucked a lemon from the tree. 'What is this called in English?'

'A lemon.'

'Ah, an elemon - that is almost the same as Spanish. We call it a *limón*. This is very interesting. We will talk more later, but now I have things to do.'

He went back down the path and we watched him turn up the *barranco*. 'Where's he going?' I said.

'Perhaps he doesn't like the look of our cactus patch and he's gone off to find a better one.'

124

While Pepe was somewhere up the *barranco* and Paco was rolling out cables, Juan did serious electrician's work. He assembled the cross bar and insulators for the pole and fiddled about with the meter box before fitting it to the wall of the kitchen. After about an hour, Pepe returned with a bundle of sticks which he dumped at the corner of the terrace. He picked one out of the bundle and came over with it. 'What is this called in English?'

'A stick,' I said.

'An estick. In Spanish it is a *leña*.' He nodded and ambled back down to the *barranco*.

'What is he doing?' I said to Linda. 'We're paying for this lot by the hour and so far all he's done is collect a few sticks and have an English lesson.'

'I don't know,' said Linda, 'maybe the wood's for a fire to heat up pitch or something.'

Paco had finished rolling out the cables and Juan told him to chop down the white cedar that was in the way.

'But Juan, that isn't our tree,' I pointed out.

'Do you want electricity?'

While Paco cut down the tree, Juan looked for the best place to erect the pole. It had to be high enough above the *barranco* to avoid being washed away in the event of flooding.

'Put it here at the end of our field,' I said.

Juan measured the distance with his eye. 'That's too far from the pole at Los Morales. It will have to be on the other side of the *barranco*.'

'But we don't own those fields.' This time, Juan didn't bother to answer. Yes, Juan, we do want

125

electricity, but we'd also like to be speaking to our neighbours. Neither Bernardo and Carmela, nor Adela and Fra'quito were at home to ask for advice and I decided to let matters take their course.

Juan told Paco to dig the hole for the power pole in the corner of a field that had not been cultivated since we arrived. The field was owned by a family who lived in Cordoba and I just prayed that they were nothing to do with Fra'quito and Adela. I was still trying to reconcile the loss of a tree from one neighbour's field and the addition of a power pole to another's, when I arrived back on the terrace. Pepe had used his bundle of sticks to make a fire in the outdoor fireplace and was sprinkling salt on to a pile of fish. Linda had laid the table and was pouring glasses of wine. It was 9.45 in the morning and, even allowing for the normal chaos of trying to get anything done in Andalucía, things here seemed to be totally out of control.

'He did ask,' said Linda.

'I don't care. We're going to be charged for him being their chef. Well, I'm not paying and I'm going to talk to Juan.'

Juan and Paco arrived on the terrace. They were in good humour; it was ten o'clock and time to eat. Pepe offered us some of the fish. 'We'd better not have any,' I said. 'They'll probably charge us for it.' I turned to Juan and gestured towards Pepe. 'What exactly is his role in this job?'

'The old one? He's my father. He gets bored at home so I let him come along with us. He gets in the way if he tries to help, but he cooks good fish.'

Linda gave me one of her look-what-a-fool-you-are

expressions, which she had become something of an expert at, and I tucked into my fish. Juan was right – it *was* good.

I pointed at a stick that had fallen out of the fireplace. 'Pepe,' I said, 'what's that called in English?'

Pepe furrowed his brow and stared hard at the stick. 'Ah, *si, si,*' he said at last triumphantly, 'I have got it - an escrewdriver.'

The issue of our neighbours' fields that had been rearranged by Juan *la Luz* was not resolved until the following summer. The owner of the field that was now decorated with a power pole paid us a visit in August. He was on holiday from Cordoba with his family and, inevitably, he was Adela's cousin. He caught me at a bad moment. It was a ferociously hot afternoon and I was rebuilding a section of the front wall of the house, balanced on a ladder trying to position heavy rocks while I filled in the surrounding gaps with mud. The only place I wanted to be was the beach.

I discovered him standing at the bottom of the ladder scowling up at me, his feet wide apart and his hands deep in his pockets. He baldly demanded one hundred thousand pesetas compensation for the loss of his valuable land - approximately one square yard in the corner of the field - otherwise we must remove the pole. I knew that the market value of the whole field was less than two hundred thousand pesetas and his demand was a blatant attempt at blackmail.

'One hundred thousand pesetas?' I said in disbelief. 'If you want that much money you'd better talk to Juan *la Luz* and see if he'll give it to you, because

I won't. I'll give you ten thousand and not a peseta more.'

'Then you must take down your pole and put it somewhere else.'

I swear that what happened next was an accident. The rock I had been holding in position slipped in my grasp and toppled from the wall. It thudded onto the ground between his straddled legs. He looked down at the rock and back up at me. Neither of us spoke. We stared at each other for several moments, and he must have seen something in my eyes that made him glance up at the row of loose rocks on top of the wall and move hurriedly away from the foot of the ladder.

'And don't touch that pole or I'll go to the police,' I said to his departing back.

Several days later I gave Adela ten thousand pesetas to give to her cousin. She agreed it was fair compensation and said that she would talk to him. The only time I saw her cousin again was in Castell plaza shortly before he went back to Cordoba. He nodded curtly to me and made no mention of either the ten thousand pesetas or the pole.

Our other neighbour whose land had been reorganised by Juan *la Luz* was an old friend of José Manzano and now lived in Granada. We went to see him while he was visiting his family in Los Carlos. He declined our offer of compensation for the loss of his tree.

'You have saved me a job,' he said. 'It was getting much too big and for some time I'd been thinking I should do something about it.' He smiled. 'Perhaps I should be paying *you*.'

'What a really nice man,' Linda said as we drove back up the *rambla.*

'Yes, North Pole - South Pole,' I said, trying to be enigmatic.

CHAPTER ELEVEN

It is only when you live without electricity that you find out how truly vital it is. After Juan *la Luz* installed power to the *cortijo* our lives were transformed. Electric lighting extended our days beyond sunset and we no longer fumbled around, tired and irritable, in the gloom at the end of the day preparing meals, and we could actually see what we were eating - we had discovered that enforced candlelit dinners soon become strangely unromantic. We read in the evenings without eyestrain; we no longer walked around the house with a hurricane lamp in one hand, or groped under the pillow for a torch to investigate rustlings in the night. We nonchalantly flicked switches - just for the novelty of seeing the lights come on - and we could at last use the electric pump to fill the water tanks. No more emptying the chemical toilet and washing in a bowl; we had a shower, a flushing toilet, and a tap at the kitchen sink. I could use my electric drill - I had learnt that toiling away with a brace and bit was carrying self-sufficiency too far - and jobs that had taken me an hour now took minutes. We toyed with the idea of buying a television, but enticing though the prospect was of spending our evenings watching badly-dubbed repeats of *Starsky and Hutch*, we resisted the temptation.

Spring arrived and, armed with our recently acquired gardening skills, we set about cultivating the land. The soil was light and easy to work, something our gardening books described as friable, and far removed from our back garden in Bristol. I went to the local *cooperativo* and bought a sack of special seed potatoes which, when I inspected them back at the *cortijo*, appeared no different to the potatoes sold at Castell market for a third of the price.

In England we had turned the garden over with a fork or a spade, but these tools were unknown here. The *campesinos* used mattocks with sharpened, square blades and lightweight, almond-wood handles that had been worn smooth. I discovered an old, rounded mattock head in an outhouse and I fashioned a crude, thick handle using a branch from the white cedar. It weighed a ton, but I wielded it with enthusiasm and vigour, sending soil flying everywhere as I dug a furrow the length of the *campo*. After ten minutes of frenzied effort, my arms were like spaghetti and my back was reminding me that I was a long way from a chiropractor. I had drawn level with the spreading mandarin tree, which I suddenly realised had been positioned there for just such an emergency, and I dropped my mattock and lay down in the shade. I was about to close my eyes when I sensed a presence. I turned my head to discover Bernardo, Paco Martin, and Manolo and Antonio, the sons of two of the sisters in La Venta, standing in a silent group about ten yards away, regarding me and shaking their heads.

I jumped to my feet and glanced over my shoulder at the row I had dug. It curved like a crescent moon. Well, there's no law that says potatoes have to be planted in a straight line. Bernardo stopped shaking his head and, like a magician, produced a roll of twine from his pocket. He weighted one end with a rock, stretched it across the field at right angles to my arc, and weighted the other end. It was so simple ... so obvious. Why hadn't I done that? He picked up my mattock, looked at the rounded, blunt end, felt the weight of the handle, and put it down again. Paco Martin handed him his mattock and, with short, chopping strokes, the seventy-five-year-old Bernardo fashioned a perfectly straight, slightly raised row, in what seemed like about four seconds.

'Why not that way?' I said, pointing to my furrow.

'Because your *campo* slopes downhill to the *barranco*,' said Bernardo. 'You must have your rows widthways. To irrigate, you start at the top and direct the water from one row to the next until it reaches the bottom. If your rows were lengthways you would be able to water only the first row. The water could not flow back up the *campo* and it would run into the *barranco* and be lost.'

'Water does not flow uphill,' contributed Paco Martin.

'I know that,' I said, 'I just didn't think about it.'

'Then it is just as well we are here,' said Paco Martin.

Bernardo inspected several of my seed potatoes. He read the label on the sack. '*Cuanto vale?*'

I told him how much they had cost me and he tossed one to Paco, who looked at it and laughed. I started to take the potatoes and place them at nine-inch intervals in Bernardo's row. I knew from Matt Ashford's immaculate vegetable garden in Bristol that this was the right spacing. The group shook its collective head and Bernardo picked one of the potatoes out of the row. He opened his knife and cut it in half.

'*Patatas* need two eyes to grow from. Look at this.' He held the two halves an inch from my nose. 'This *patata* has five eyes. It will not produce any more if you plant it whole; so now you will get twice the crop.'

I cut some of the potatoes, making sure that I had at least two eyes on each piece and once again I started to place them in the row. I looked round for approval but they were tutting.

'No,' said Bernardo, 'you have to leave the pieces in the air to harden. If you put them in the earth freshly cut they will rot. Also it is the wrong time to plant them.'

'It is lucky for you we're here to help,' observed Paco Martin.

'But the man in the *cooperativo* said to plant them now.'

'*Si,* but in the *ninguante* not the *creciente*,' said Bernardo.

'Also, it would have been cheaper to buy your *patatas* from the market,' added Paco Martin helpfully.

Manolo and Antonio nodded in agreement. They had contributed little to my lesson in Andalucían agriculture, instead deferring to the superior knowledge of their elders, although I felt sure that if

133

Bernardo and Paco Martin hadn't been there they would have been more vocal. What had started off as a happy hour in the field planting a row of potatoes had now become unbelievably complicated. Linda was on the terrace and I called to her to bring down the dictionary.

'They're ganging up on me and they won't let me plant these spuds.'

Linda came down with the dictionary. '*Creciente* is the waxing moon and *ninguante* is the waning moon,' she said.

'Are they serious? Surely it doesn't make any difference.'

Bernardo understood from my tone what I'd said. He explained, as if to a child. 'In the *creciente* sap rises and plants grow big and strong above the ground.' He raised himself to his full height of five feet four inches and thrust out his thin chest. 'But in the *ninguante* sap falls and plants grow strongly below the ground.' He bent at the knees and dropped his shoulders. 'So, when you plant your *patatas* in the *ninguante* they grow big and have *mucho vigor.*' He stood up straight again and managed to look vigorous.

'It is obvious,' said Paco Martin. 'If you eat what is beneath the earth you plant in the *ninguante*. If you eat what is above the earth you plant in the *creciente*.'

'Also,' said Bernardo, not to be outdone, 'you cut the canes for the ceilings and the white cedar for the roof beams in January in the *ninguante*. You want as little sap as possible, otherwise the insects will bore into them and they will turn to powder.'

I looked at Linda; our efforts in Bristol had not

prepared us for any of this. The word quickly went out that I was utterly incompetent in the *campo* and I dreaded going down there. I knew that the moment I lifted my mattock someone would materialise from the shadow of a tree and spend ten minutes telling me what I was doing wrong. Paco Martin was the worst. His advice consisted of crushing discouragement designed to make me believe we would be better off buying our vegetables at the market, which was ironic because his field was the only unkempt one around. I learnt that his fee for this advice was several glasses of wine, regardless of the time of day. He lived halfway to Castell, in an old *cortijo* with his brother, and travelled to his field at Los Morales on an ancient Bultaco motorbike. It was low to the ground and unsuitable for the terrain, and the footrests hit every rock as it chugged up the *rambla*. Before I went into the *campo,* I took to climbing the hill behind the house to scan the neighbouring fields. If I couldn't see anyone I'd hurry down, hoping that I could get half-an-hour's work done before I was discovered, and always ready to dash back to the house if I heard footsteps in the *barranco,* or an approaching *moto* - especially one with scraping footrests.

But the advice from Bernardo, José, Adela, and so many of our other neighbours was priceless and given generously, with only the desire to help. They could not bear to watch us make such a mess of things that, to them, were second nature. As a result, we had a bumper crop of potatoes, not in the same league as José's mountain when we arrived, but good enough to show off to him. Linda dedicated a lot of manure and

135

compost to the onion row and produced giants. The largest weighed more than two and a half pounds and we were tempted to parcel it up and send it to the Bristol Show. By the end of our first growing season we knew that if, like the locals, we ate what was in season we could be virtually self sufficient. Some of the vegetables we grew stored well and we had strings of garlic, onions and dried chillies hanging from the walls in the kitchen, potatoes in hessian sacks and root vegetables in boxes of sand. We considered buying a freezer, but we lost our electricity after anything stronger than a stiff breeze, and following major storms we could be without power for up to a week until an electricity company truck meandered up the *rambla* repairing the lines.

We had many failures. Our exotic seeds that we had brought out from England struggled and gave a terrible return. We experimented with chicory, asparagus peas, kohlrabi and a variety of lettuces. They produced stunted, deformed plants that we tried to hide from our neighbours. The seeds had been intended for the English climate and, even in spring, the heat here was more than the plants could stand. We planted a row of Brussels sprouts that never grew larger than marbles, our perpetual spinach bolted the moment the sun came out; a mid-summer crop of tomatoes cooked on the plants; and a patch of wheat for the chickens did not produce enough to feed them for a week.

The locals didn't experiment. They had grown the same vegetables for generations and knew what did well. In addition to the *habichuelas*, which were their main commercial crop, they grew stock-standard vegetables for the table: tomatoes, peppers, courgettes, aubergines, onions, garlic, potatoes, broad beans and carrots. They never altered the varieties - they simply saved the seeds from the strongest plants - and the women cooked the vegetables in exactly the same ways that their mothers and grandmothers had. In this region, change came slowly.

We had a rare success with mange-tout peas, which our neighbours had never seen before. We explained that they were the same as ordinary peas except that you ate the pods as well, just like their runner beans. They were sceptical and looked at the plants suspiciously. We gave some to Adela and Carmela, but neither said if they liked them and it occurred to us that they probably fed them straight to their goats.

Working in the *campo*, I was continually reminded of the civil war. Hardly a week went by when I didn't find a .303 cartridge - a long brass cylinder that even without a bullet in the end looked dangerous. The war had been over for more than forty years, but I dug up dozens of them. I wondered who had stood with their rifles in our field and for which side they had fought. What had they been firing at for there to be this many cartridges? There was Los Morales opposite; perhaps Franco's soldiers had surrounded it - a small contingent in our field and another contingent behind Los Morales in the *rambla* - a net closing in on Bernardo's house. But our field was too exposed to provide much protection; it was not a place for soldiers to stage an ambush. It was more likely a place where they themselves had been ambushed, maybe as they were leaving Los Sanchez and they had returned the enemy fire - the ridge above the Rubité road was the perfect spot to have lain in wait for them. But none of it rang true. I decided it was more likely that a group of soldiers had lined up a row of bottles on the ridge, walked down to our *campo* and shot at them for target practice.

José called round one day when I was in the field and I showed him several of the cartridges. The previous times I had asked him about the war he had not wanted to discuss it; it was something that no one who had fought in was keen to relive. But that day the valley was still; Andalucía was dozing in the heat of the afternoon and the guns were a long way off. He held one of the cartridges between his thumb and index finger and shook the earth out of it.

'*Hombre*, here in this region there was bad fighting - although I did not see it. I was stationed in the north and learnt of it only after I came back when the war was over. Come with me; I will show you something.'

I went with him to the earth cliffs alongside the *rambla* close to La Venta. He stood beside me and pointed. 'Look at those caves. Now they are easy to see, but they were once hidden by grass and shrubs. Men from both sides hid in them during the war, sometimes for weeks, and the women and the children brought them food. Everybody knew they were there except the people who were looking for them.'

We walked closer; the cliffs were sheer, but earth falls had built up at the base, allowing us to scramble up to the lowest cave. It was the size of a small room and smelt of animals. It had been hollowed out of the red earth, with a domed roof and walls that sloped inwards. The roof was low - there was barely enough room to stand upright at the highest point - and it was a network of fractures. We stepped over slabs of earth that had fallen from the roof and lay intact on the floor. The thought of spending weeks in here, faced with the very real possibility that the roof would collapse, was terrifying - we weren't five feet in from the entrance and I was feeling claustrophobic - but, if the only alternative was the certainty of being shot, then I suppose I could have got used to it.

José walked with me back to the *cortijo* and we talked of other things. I had hoped to hear more about how the war had affected the region, but even after forty years it was too close. People could not forget the atrocities; they still counted the cost of a war in which there was no common enemy, where three-quarters of a million Spaniards died, and men from the same hamlets fought each other and afterwards had to live side by side. The wounds were slowly healing and there was nothing to be gained by reopening them - it was best left alone.

CHAPTER TWELVE

Despite the atrocious roads and the small population living in the foothills of the Alpujarras, traders made regular deliveries to the hamlets, which the people depended upon. Invariably, their arrival was heralded by prolonged horn-blasting, which we had initially believed to be nothing more than a noisy expression of Spanish exuberance. It wasn't until we saw women emerge from their houses, or from where they had been working in the fields, and make their way to a muster point that we realised something was about to happen. In addition to these anticipated deliveries, there were random traders who hawked their produce throughout the region and occasionally found their way to our *cortijo*. They generally arrived by mule or on foot and would silently hold out a bundle of onion seedlings or a handful of small, hard goats' cheeses, or other items they had grown or made themselves.

Periodically, a man walked up the *rambla* leading a jangling donkey, its halter covered with bells and coloured tassels. The donkey had a woven reed pannier on either flank, with the heads of pink, squirming piglets peering over the top. Adela bought a piglet from him once a year. She kept it in a small *corral*, fattening it up into a 300 pound monster until the fateful day of the *matanza* – the pig killing. A few months after we arrived we heard Adela's pig being slaughtered. We were still in bed and the noise continued for fifteen minutes. We held our pillows over our ears and vowed we would never keep a pig, although when Little Adela came round four days later with a plate of pork and exquisite homemade sausages our resolve wavered.

Pigs are intelligent and likable animals, and over the course of the year the families become attached to them. Because of this, the task of killing the animal is taken on by someone outside the family, often on a reciprocal basis. It is done at first light during the winter. The men of the family stand in a huddle knocking back *aguardiente* - a cheap spirit made from figs - for warmth and courage. When they are sufficiently fortified, the slaughterer produces his long, slim knife, the men hold the animal, and he inserts the blade. Their work over, the men spend the rest of the morning enjoying more *aguardiente* while the women gut the animal, remove and wash the intestines, scrape off all the hair and scrub the carcass, before hanging it for 24 hours or so until the flesh firms. After the pig has finished hanging, there is the *matanza* party, to which all the relatives and friends are invited. It is called a party, but essentially it is a party only for the men. In reality, the women spend the day working and the men spend the day drinking.

The first *matanza* party we were invited to was at Virtruda and Manolo's house at La Venta. The women arrived with knives and choppers and mincers, and immediately disappeared into Virtruda's kitchen to process about 200 pounds of meat. The four legs were trimmed and packed in salt, before being taken high into the Alpujarras, where they were destined to hang in the mountain air for several months to be transformed into *serrano* hams. The blood was cooked and used as the filling for *morcilla* sausages, and pounds and pounds of meat and fat were minced and blended with herbs and spices, and the mixtures stuffed into yards of cleaned intestines, as the women made strings of *chorizo, longaniza* and *salchichon* sausages. Meat was preserved in jars of salt and oil, and choice pieces put aside to be distributed among the helpers. In mid morning, I stuck my head around the kitchen door and quickly retreated. It was a cross between an abattoir and my image of the debtor's prison in *Little Dorrit*.

While all the women, including Linda, were in the kitchen labouring and bonding, the men congregated around a fire on the three sisters' huge communal terrace, with a cigarette in one hand and a drink in the other. Transferring the cigarettes to their mouths, they took it in turns to stir an enormous pot containing the pig's offal and fatty bits of meat, dozens of potatoes, tied bunches of thyme and oregano and about fifty whole bulbs of garlic - a truly prodigious amount - the whole lot floating around in an equal quantity of water and olive oil. Every now and then one of the sisters would come out and throw more meat into the pot.

Mari-Carmen's fiancé, Paco, had taken it upon himself to look after me and keep me supplied with drinks. He was drinking *Cuba libre*, a mixture of cola and *ron* - a dark rum made in Motril from the local sugar cane - and quite a sophisticated drink for the *rambla*. It was going to be a long day and I decided to be sensible, keep clear of spirits and stick to *vino costa*. By early afternoon, the stew that all morning I had viewed with suspicion was adjudged by the men to be ready. We helped ourselves, ladling it into massive bowls, and using it to soften chunks of Gonzo's bread. The stew had become thick and rich and, despite my doubts, tasted extraordinarily good. By this time, I was well into my second bottle of *costa* and something seemed to be happening to my lips. Whatever it was spread to my mouth and cheeks. I prodded the area with my finger and discovered that this entire region of my face had become anaesthetized. It was a very strange thing to have happened - it was as though I'd been to the dentist. For the rest of the afternoon I sat with Francisco *Alcalde*, Paco, and the three cousins, drinking *costa* and talking incoherently about I know not what.

Late in the afternoon, Linda emerged from the kitchen. She had spent most of the day standing while she turned the handle of an oversized mincer and was desperate to sit down with a glass of wine. She listened to me for a few seconds and abruptly announced that we were leaving. It was not a tone to be argued with but, to my astonishment, I found that my legs had also been anaesthetized. Linda nodded grimly to Paco and, with the same ease that he lifted the sacks of *habichuelas* on to the back of his truck, he put me across his shoulder and carried me to the van. Linda drove home without speaking to me and poured me into bed. Personally, I blame all that garlic.

The truck carrying the orange cylinders of *butano* gas called with unfailing regularity on the first Tuesday of the month. It stopped in the *rambla* at the bottom of Los Morales and the tranquillity was shattered as the driver leant on his horn until either Adela or I emerged with an empty cylinder. If no one appeared after five minutes he took his hand off the horn and drove two hundred yards onto the Rubité road and stopped at the top of Los Morales outside Bernardo and Carmela's house, where he repeated the procedure. The driver came from Motril and every time I spoke to him he would say how peaceful it was where we lived.

The delivery of *cal* - the quicklime rocks from which whitewash is made - arrived on the back of an open-sided truck once a year to coincide with the saint day on which the women whitewashed their houses - a day on which, at some distant point in time, someone had decreed that all houses in the land be whitewashed. Now, it was as though the task of whitewashing had acquired a common brain and to have done it at any other time would have been like celebrating Christmas in March. For weeks after the ritualistic whitewashing, the hamlets and the villages were blindingly white, sparkling as if they had been coated with icing, until dust and rain gradually dulled them.

Cal is dangerous. The rocks are dropped into water, which instantly starts to bubble and heave, and soon is a seething, spitting mass, like the primeval formation of the earth. The mixture is highly caustic and the heat generated is astonishing. At my first

144

attempt I melted a plastic bucket and the next time I used a metal dustbin with a lid. After twelve hours the reaction is over and it is safe to dilute and use.

The women painted their houses with round toilet brushes. They tied a bamboo cane to the handle for the high sections and spread out ancient, tattered sheets at the base of the walls. They wrapped scarves around their faces and wore yellow rubber gloves and long, pastel smocks, which I never saw at any other time. Both the sheets and the women became caked with whitewash and I fully understood why the men had decided this was women's work.

Several weeks after we arrived, we were visited by a small van with a large black loudspeaker mounted on its roof. It came down the Rubité road and we heard it long before it became visible. The same few words were repeated at immense volume, distorted beyond recognition. The echoes were trapped in the valley and bounced around the hillsides, overlapping and merging until they became a paralysing madhouse of noise. Our immediate reaction was that the vehicle was touring the mountains campaigning for the upcoming elections in Rubité, and we stood and watched it with our fingers in our ears. It halted at the top of Los Morales and the noise gradually died away. Adela emerged from her house as the driver got out and opened the back doors of the van. He looked across at us and while he waited for Adela he reached into the cab, pulled out the microphone and bellowed, '*PATOS, PAVOS Y POLLOS*' Just what we wanted - DUCKS, TURKEYS AND CHICKENS. We ran down the front path, crossed the *barranco,* and scrambled up the track to the top of Los Morales.

The back of the van was filled with cages of domestic fowl, ranging from fluffy day-old chicks to heavy-bodied brown turkeys with evil expressions and wobbling jowls. Adela was concluding negotiations to buy four small, sturdy turkeys that looked as though they'd be a handful when they got older. We came away with thirteen *pollitos* - tiny, five-day-old chickens. We had asked for a dozen, queried his price, and he'd thrown in another, free. They were unkempt grey birds, with spiteful expressions, that pecked at anything within range and needed to be kept inside for two weeks until they were large enough to forage in the field and survive the cool nights. The man sold us a sack of chick feed and told us to stir it into warm water until it became a thick pulpy porridge. It had an unpleasant, fishy smell.

In the low-ceilinged attic, directly above our bedroom, was a small enclosure with concrete walls and a rough stone floor that had desiccated remains of bird droppings. The thirteen chicks remained there for almost a fortnight. We fed them ceaselessly, listened to their mutterings at night, broke up their squabbles during the day, and bent double to clean up their guano while they pecked at our hands. They were like thirteen bed-bound, demanding and ungrateful house guests. After a week their smell had penetrated to our bedroom and, by the end, had invaded the whole house.

'They smell foul.'

'They are fowl.'

'Nevertheless,' said Linda, 'either they go, or I do.'

The next day I moved the chicks out of the attic into a stone *corral* in the field. They had trebled in size and now seemed capable of surviving outside. José wandered over as I was feeding them grain.

'Fattening them up for Christmas?'

'No, we're keeping them for the eggs. We'll get a lot more than we need and we're going to barter with them.'

'That will be a miracle,' said José, 'those are cockerels.' Somehow, he kept a straight face. 'You have bought *pollitos*. You needed to buy *gallinas*.'

I broke the news to Linda. 'I never did like them,' she said, 'the way they kept pecking our hands and fighting each other. I should have known they were males.'

As they grew bigger they turned vicious and roamed the field in a pack. The half-wild ginger cat, which had come with the *cortijo,* eyed them up when we first bought them, but soon gave them a wide berth. One day, the ringleader came up behind Linda as she was stretching to hang clothes on the line and pecked her calf muscle. She came back to the house in a rage, with blood streaming down her leg. They were the only animals that I had little compunction in killing, and we ate the first one when my brother, Neil, visited in February. He came on his own; he was reconnoitring to find out if it was safe for Lesley and their two young children, and to confirm his earlier judgement that we were mad.

Christmas had been cold, wet and lonely; we had missed our family and friends and we were delighted to see him. We honoured his visit with the cockerel that had attacked Linda. It was nothing like the pallid English supermarket chickens that always seemed to taste of fish. The meat was yellow and had a strong, gamey flavour - with a sweet lingering aftertaste of revenge.

Approximately twice a month, Juan, a vigneron from a nearby coastal village, journeyed up the *rambla*. His open-sided truck was filled with onion-shaped carboys containing five gallons of wine. The carboys were made of thick green glass and sat in two-handled reed baskets that were stained dirty red and smelled of vinegar. His best customers were the *muleros*. Theirs was the hardest and loneliest job of all - work that took a huge toll on their bodies as they slogged behind the mules, forcing the ploughs through rocks and shale, high on the slopes. We often saw the *muleros* from the back of our house, specks amongst the almond trees on the distant hillsides - being pursued by trails of dust. They might not see another person from the time they left their homes at dawn until they returned at dusk, when they collapsed and drank themselves into oblivion. We knew two *muleros* - Antonio, the son of Fra'quito and Adela, and another Antonio, who lived close to José Manzano. Sometimes, late in the day, we met one of them as he trudged down the mule path alongside our *cortijo*, coated in dust and too tired to talk. They both hated their work and were legendary drinkers.

The first time we saw Juan, he had parked his truck in the *rambla* at the junction with the *barranco* and was sounding the horn. It was early afternoon and we went down to investigate. Juan had dropped the tailgate and set up a line of bottles, turning the rusty bed of his truck into a bar. We stood in the *rambla,* with the sun warming our backs, as Juan led us through his selection of wines. These were no ordinary tastings we were given, but half-tumblers full. We started with a dust-dry fino and worked our way, in gradual stages, up to a huge, muscular red. Juan handed a glass to Linda. *'Sangre de toro,'* he said and gestured towards his testicles. Bull's blood! I'd always wanted to try it.

Linda took a sip and winced. 'Good God.'

She passed me her glass and Juan laughed. I know it isn't possible, but it tasted stronger than cognac. It burnt my tongue, cleared my sinuses, tore at the lining of my throat, and I'm sure it dissolved everything it touched on its way to my stomach. It probably had a handy industrial use, but I don't believe you could have drunk five gallons of it and lived.

Juan had stood looking into the sun, his face glowing mightily, and with obvious enjoyment he had matched us drink for drink while he described the qualities of his wines. During the course of his days on the road he must have drunk a fair portion of his produce and profit, and his philosophy made me think of the lines from Omar Khayyam in which he wonders what vintners could possibly buy that is half as precious as the goods they sell.

We settled for a carboy of *vino costa,* the wine of the region, made in every village from whatever grapes are available - a pot-luck wine ranging in taste and body from a medium sherry to a delicate rosé. From what I could remember at that stage of the tasting, Juan's *costa* had been red and fruity - a good wine for

149

most occasions. Linda suggested we buy just a couple of bottles, rather than five gallons, but the cost was so dramatically less by buying in bulk that I pooh-poohed the idea.

'Look at it this way,' I said, with the logic of the inebriated, 'it's a simple matter of economics. The more we drink, the more we save.'

I've always found that wine tastes better at a bodega or winery than it ever does when you get it home, and Juan's *costa* was no different. That evening, with the meal, it tasted flat and uninspiring and we thought it was because the bull's blood had obliterated our taste buds. But it didn't improve and, despite our most determined efforts, the wine oxidised before we finished it. It developed strange tastes after a week and caused us to spend a lot of the next morning in the loo. We relegated it to cooking use until, eventually, it became too disgusting even for that and we poured it away.

'We should have invited the two Antonios round,' Linda said, 'they'd have demolished it in an evening.'

One day, for no logical reason, José went out and bought three nanny goats. He lived by himself and, on his own admission, disliked milk. He was cultivating lentils and lucerne in La Marina's field and he had as many labouring jobs as he could handle. Goats are a lot of work, which is shared by a whole family. They have to be milked every day, kept fed and watered, locked up at night and watched over while they browse, because if you aren't careful they will go into a neighbour's field and demolish his crops, or in our case, almond saplings. For us, it was wonderful. The shops in Castell stocked long-life milk, which tasted like milk of magnesia, and just one supermarket in Motril had a delivery of fresh milk once a week, which was sold out by mid-morning. The long-life milk was packaged in tough tetra-pack cartons but, illogically, the fresh milk was sold in polythene bags and, even if we were lucky enough to buy some in Motril, there was a good chance it would not survive the journey back up the *rambla*. José came every morning with his goats and called up to the house from the edge of our field. Linda ran down with a saucepan and José squirted milk into it while the goats docilely chewed the grass. José's goats had a thoroughly objectionable smell, but their milk was thick, sweet and odourless. We made yoghurt that tasted like ice cream and soft cheeses that were as smooth and creamy as butter.

Brucellosis is endemic to the region and transmitted by un-pasteurised milk. The procedure to pasteurise milk is quick and simple; although on the first few occasions we stood together by the stove as the milk heated, consulted the self-sufficiency book and continually checked the temperature with a thermometer to make sure it remained constant for the required period. After a while, pasteurising José's milk became simply a matter of routine. The procedure to obtain the milk in the first place was far more complicated and one we never mastered, despite the many occasions that José tried to teach us. We watched him as he kneaded and pulled the teats until the milk came out in a strong jet, but whenever Linda or I tried to do it nothing happened. The goats stood patiently while we pummelled and tugged and squeezed, without ever extracting a drop, until finally they'd had enough and kicked over the saucepan.

Several times a year a truck selling linen, towels and blankets ground its way up the *rambla*. It stopped at every hamlet, where the driver and his assistant set up trestle tables to display their wares. The women loved these goods and the fields emptied as crowds gathered. The prize items were encased in cellophane - delicate, crocheted tablecloths, embroidered bedspreads, fine cotton sheets and pillowcases with lace edging, and vast, fluffy towels - all in pure white. We wondered who bought these things - in our house they would not have remained white for a day- until one afternoon Francisco *Alcalde* and Madelena's daughter, Mari-Carmen, showed us the contents of a chest in her bedroom. Her trousseau consisted almost entirely of merchandise from the truck.

But they did not just sell items for young girls' trousseaux. There was something for everyone - combed nylon bedspreads in bold jungle patterns with prowling tigers, their teeth bared to protect the sleeper; thin blankets in sludgy checks; crocheted tablecloths in sensible fawn; and rough towels in washed-out pastels. There was a separate trestle table for the display of tablecloths and fabrics in sombre colours, designed specifically for the room in the house that was reserved for special occasions and important guests. These rooms were a phenomenon of the towns and villages and were less common in the remoter areas. The rooms were dusted and polished daily but rarely used; they had heavy, dark furniture, with chair covers and curtains in various shades of mud; the floors had white or grey marble tiles; and the shutters were always kept closed. On the walls, there were large gold crosses, brightly-painted plaster casts of the Virgin Mary, and framed prints of the crucifixion. The rooms resembled mausoleums. On the occasions we were ushered into them, in deference to our status as foreigners, we sat stiff and uncomfortable on the hard chairs, praying that we would not spill our drinks or drop a crumb.

We would have thought that, out of all the hawkers who plied their trade up and down the *rambla,* these sellers of home wares would have been the least likely to make a good living, but we witnessed them sell prodigious quantities - although they were one of the few traders we never bought from.

My favourite of all the hawkers was a man who rode an ancient *moto* that had a plastic milk crate strapped onto the back mudguard. He came to Los Sanchez during our first week there. He was on his way to see Adela when he spotted us on the terrace and speculatively took a detour up the *barranco*. At the halfway point he started to scream out, '*Pay...cow.*' He cut the first syllable short and extended the second into a high-pitched wail. It was the sort of noise that if you heard it at night would make you pull the covers over your head. He dismounted at the bottom of our path and walked up until he was a few paces from us. He was thin and unshaven, and was wearing a black PVC helmet lined with fake fur – of the style favoured by early aviators – with its ear flaps buttoned down onto the chin strap. He looked like Biggles fallen upon hard times.

'*Pay...cow*,' he wailed. He stared at us expectantly and we stared back at him.

He repeated his call and we shook our heads. '*No comprendo*'.

He walked back to his *moto*, rummaged in the milk crate and returned with a small sardine, its tail gripped between his thumb and forefinger. He waggled it under our noses. '*Pay...cow.*'

Of course ...*pescado* ... fish.

Even in the height of summer he wore his helmet with the flaps firmly buttoned down. If I had met him in the street without it I would not have recognised him, and if I had seen him in a line-up of assorted thin and unshaven men wearing identical headgear, I would not have been able to pick him out. He had become his helmet.

He was given a terrible time by the housewives. When he stopped at La Venta, half a dozen women huddled around the *moto*, sorting through his fish while they made disparaging remarks. The sardines were too small; they were soft; they were yesterday's catch; they were too expensive; they were not sardines at all - they were minnows. When they finally condescended to buy his sardines, he weighed them in a plastic bowl on hand-held scales of dubious accuracy, adding brass weights from his jacket pocket. Without exception, when the scales had settled, the women reached into the crate and threw a few more sardines into the bowl. One day, I saw him hurl the fish onto the ground and ride off on his *moto*, shouting curses at them as they stood in a cackling group. But he always came back and they continued to buy from him after the same merciless baiting. I once came across him miles away in another valley, at the village of Polopos. He was in the plaza, his *moto* surrounded by women, suffering identical jibes and abuse.

CHAPTER THIRTEEN

For much of the year in England, driving the van without its windscreen would have been dismal. But here, it posed few problems. The Mediterranean coast between Almeria and Malaga has no snow, very few frosts, and low rainfall. When it does rain, it is often torrential, with a quarter of the year's rain falling in the space of a few days and afterwards, for weeks on end, the sky is cloudless. In the winter, we wore our sheepskin coats - which we nearly hadn't brought with us – and, if it was raining, we followed the example of the locals and didn't move from the house. When we couldn't avoid driving in the rain, Linda sat in the back where it was dry and I wore a hooded waterproof cape and kept a box of tissues handy to wipe my glasses. Our only worry was that, if enough rain came in, it would short out the dashboard, but it never did. The Bedford seemed to be indestructible. When we parked the van in the *barranco*, we put a sheet of old plastic from the greenhouses across the windscreen, holding it in position by trapping it in the sliding doors and weighting it with rocks on the roof.

The worst thing was when we followed another

vehicle along the *rambla* and choked on its dust. We would try to get on to a parallel path or, if we weren't in a hurry, slow down or stop until they were at least half a mile ahead. The absence of the windscreen was an inconvenience, but no more so than many other aspects of our life, such as not having a washing machine, no hot water in the kitchen, enduring regular power cuts, collecting our cooking and drinking water from a spring, not having glass in the windows and, when it rained, positioning buckets under all the seemingly incurable roof leaks.

When we first parked the van in the *barranco,* everyone warned us it would be washed away. José showed me the remains of a stone *corral* at the foot of our path. 'Fifteen years ago, after a *tormenta* in the mountains, there was a wall of water in the *barranco* this high.' He held his hand above his head. 'This *corral* was smashed to pieces as if it was made from matches. Your field was under water. The *rambla* was a torrent and houses were lost. Sheep and goats and even mules were carried away, taken all the way to Castell and out to sea. So your little van would stand no chance.'

'I thought that the rainfall was much less nowadays and you don't get those storms any more.'

José shrugged. He had said what could happen; he was not going to argue about it with someone who knew nothing of his country. 'Who knows what might happen in the mountains. All it needs is one big *tormenta.*'

It was hard to imagine that the trickle which was diverted into the water deposit could ever be ferocious and destructive. Nevertheless, whenever we saw black clouds looming over the mountains behind the house, or sitting on the ridges around us, I drove the van to the top of Los Morales and parked it on the Rubité road next to Bernardo and Carmela's house. For the water to reach it there, it would first have to wash away our *cortijo* and the whole of Los Morales - and at that point we'd be past caring.

We were using the Bedford Dormobile as a commercial vehicle involved in the most degrading of tasks. It seemed to accept its role phlegmatically, but I couldn't help thinking that secretly it must have pined for its glory days. Little more than two years before it had been the headquarters of a bikini-making empire - the accommodation, restaurant and transportation of its founder and his new bride - as it mingled with the Ferraris and Porches in St Tropez. The Bedford had been well advanced in years when I bought it and who knows what exotic locations and heady adventures it had enjoyed with its previous owners. Here, it staggered up and down the *rambla,* without a windscreen and full of dust, laden with sacks of cement, bricks and other building materials; or it collected rocks from the *rambla* and pebbles from Castell beach; or else it groaned up the mountain tracks to rubbish tips where we scavenged for cast-out windows, doors and tiles, and anything else that might come in useful. Oh, the ignominy! To have sunk to this! To have become nothing more than the lowest beast of burden!

I patted it on the bonnet and resolved to give it a good clean and check the oil in the morning.

Adolfo was born in La Venta and owned a house there,

although he lived most of the year in Granada. He was a perennial student who had studied law for years while he worked part-time in a large hotel. We met him on his occasional visits to La Venta. He was urbane, spoke a dozen words of English which he used, regardless of their suitability, if other Spaniards were around, and every time we saw him he had a different girlfriend. He also had an old Ossa 250cc trail bike. This was a real motorbike, designed for the *rambla* and the steep tracks through the mountains, and was nothing like the tiny-engined *motos* that the locals putt-putted around on. He stored it in his house at La Venta and used it infrequently; his girlfriends preferring to ride in his smart car. He asked me if I wanted to buy it.

My experience of motorcycling was limited to a Lambretta scooter I owned when I was a sixteen-year-old mod. I decked it out with a mass of chrome, as was the fashion in those days, fitting shiny front and rear crash-bars and carry-racks, and a padded chrome backrest for my non-existent girlfriend to recline against. In a moment of insanity, I bolted on an aerial and attached a fox tail to the top. I wore a khaki parka with a fur-lined hood and rode the scooter in a trendy slouch. Basically, both the scooter and I looked pitiful. With a group of friends, I went to places like Yarmouth at Bank Holiday weekends and exchanged pleasantries on the beach with motorbike-riding rockers, who wore leather jackets and a lot of Brylcreem. There was a large contingent of police present on these occasions to ensure fair play.

But this was entirely different. The Ossa was a functional machine. It was a barely-street-legal motocross bike with large knobbly tyres and high ground clearance and soft suspension to cope with rocks and potholes. It would get us into Castell in a third of the time it took the Bedford, and we could explore all those rough mountain tracks that defeated the van, and discover fairytale villages hidden away in secret valleys. We bought it.

It was the best of bikes. It was the worst of bikes. Some bikes are clean, but the Ossa was filthy; it leaked oil from the engine, the gearbox, the manifold, and the front forks - and in vast quantities. It was impossible to get on the bike without being streaked black from the knees down. It sprayed sooty particles out of the exhaust, which the rear wheel threw up onto back of the rider or pillion passenger. The engine was high compression, which meant that I had to jump on the kick-start to turn it over. But there was a fault. Periodically, the kick-start failed to engage with the engine and went straight to the floor without resistance. When this happened, there was a real risk that I would break my ankle. More often than not, when it was wet, my foot slipped off the kick-start about halfway down its travel, with the result that the lever sprang back and cracked me on the shin. But by far the most infuriating thing about the Ossa was its habit of refusing to start, usually when we were ten miles from home and for no obvious reason, or else it died halfway up the *rambla*, on a hot day when we had a backpack full of shopping. I carried two spare sparkplugs against this contingency, and my initial treatment was to change the plug and check that the new one was sparking. If the bike still didn't start, I took the carburettor apart and checked that the filter wasn't clogged with dust. When that didn't work, I ran along with the Ossa until we reached a fair speed and then leapt on, jammed it into gear and prayed that the engine would fire. I had the strength to do that five or six times before I sank to my knees, groaning. After I recovered, I changed the spark plug again and repeated the whole procedure. Then I swore at the Ossa and kicked its tyres. Finally, I just stood and swore at it. Linda bought me Robert Pirsig's *Zen and the Art of Motorcycle Maintenance,* in which the author tranquilly deals with the problems to his motorbike during a journey through America. She hoped that I would learn something about motorcycle repairs, or at least approach them with a degree of equanimity. But Pirsig's book didn't help. I continued to rage at the Ossa and never understood its innards.

On its good days it was sublime. It treated the rocks and the holes and the steepest, most slippery tracks with disdain. It took us high into the Alpujarras to Trevélez - famous for its *serrano* hams and hand-woven rugs - on what is said to be the highest road in Spain, where the air is cold and, unprepared, we froze. We explored mule paths that led to abandoned hamlets and occasionally we came across one that was perfectly preserved. It was as if the owners were inside having their siesta, and at any moment they would open their front doors and emerge into the sunlight, stretching and rubbing their eyes. It took us far along the coast, down tracks to the shore, where we discovered tiny settlements, the houses so close to the water's edge that women cast lines from their balconies, and then pegged the filleted and salted fish on their clothes lines to dry. We raced up the corkscrewing dirt road to Rubité, and onwards along the ridge to the restaurant at Haza de Lino for a lunch of their wonderful kid casserole - followed by a slow and cautious ride home down the mountain. On those glorious days it was the best of bikes.

We soon became aware of the inordinate number of people in the area with disabilities. Each community had one or two simpletons and everywhere there were people with hunch backs, gammy legs, bad hearing, cleft palates, harelips, twisted faces, stammers, stutters, squints, cross eyes, cross expressions and just about anything else you care to think of. The pavements in the poorer areas of Motril resembled crowd scenes from Goya's paintings. Benny put it down to in-breeding and poor diet, but it seemed to us that many of the afflictions were minor and in wealthier parts of Europe would have been cured at a young age, but in this region of Spain medical facilities had either not been available or affordable and, untreated, the people continued to suffer.

Our community had its share of the disabled, one of whom caused us many problems over a period of several months. The three sisters in La Venta were really four, although they never spoke about the fourth. José told us that she lived somewhere in the north. She was reputed to be mad and spent her time in and out of institutions. She had a son, Miguel, a hulking, simple-minded boy about nineteen, who lived equally with the three sisters at La Venta as they shared the task of looking after him. The men often brought him with them into the fields and occasionally I saw him helping, but the work did not hold his attention for long and much of the time the men left him to his own devices. If he was in the fields close to us he would sit and watch our house. Initially, he kept his distance, but he was fascinated by us and gradually he became bolder. I would come across him at the bottom of our path or skulking behind shrubs on the hillside above us. At first it was nothing more than a minor irritation, but one day I caught Miguel concealed behind the fig tree close to the house, spying on Linda as she sunbathed in a bikini on the terrace. I shouted and chased him away, and later that day I went to La Venta and spoke to Francisco *Alcalde*. He apologised and said that the family would try to keep him away from us.

For a week we didn't see him and then one morning, when I was working in the field, I heard a noise from the house and saw him clambering across the roof. When he realised that I'd spotted him he climbed down and ran off. A few days later we came back from Castell and found that someone had broken into the house through the upstairs balcony door, which could be accessed only via the roof. Nothing was taken but drawers were open and some of Linda's clothes were spread out on the bed. The second time he broke in, two weeks later, he left his identity card on the table. Again nothing was missing, but he had ransacked drawers and cupboards. In the kitchen, he had struck a whole box of matches and the spent matches littered the floor.

'We have to go to the police.'

'I don't know that we can,' I said. 'He's not all there. If they charged him with trespass or housebreaking; they'd send him away to an institution like his mother and I hate to think of the conditions in those places.'

'Well, we have to do something.'

'Yes, but I don't think that's the solution. I'm sure we'd be condemned by the community if we went to the police. But, apart from that, can you imagine the procedure to get anything done, the visits to the police station, the forms and the statements, and then going to court - all with the language problem? We could write off the next three months. This is something we have to sort out ourselves. I'll talk to the family again.'

I returned Miguel's identity card to Francisco *Alcalde* and told him about the matches. He promised that they would stop him. But of course they couldn't. The only way they could have stopped him was if they had kept him in chains.

After that, we were all the time looking around, expecting to find him hiding somewhere watching us, and when we went out we wondered whether we would come home to find our possessions strewn about, or worse, the house burnt to the ground. We took all the boxes of matches with us when we left the house. One day he discovered that he could overcome the locked doors on the Bedford Dormobile simply by climbing in through the open windscreen. He used the van as a play house, and set up the folding table and laid out pots and pans. I removed the gas cooker and prayed that he wouldn't drop a match into the fuel tank. It was all very sad, but he was making life intolerable for us.

164

One afternoon we were working inside the house when I heard Adela shrieking from Los Morales. I went out to the terrace, and she pointed above me and screamed, '*Arriba! Arriba!*'

I looked up and saw that Miguel was again on our roof. He was scrambling to get down, in his hurry dislodging tiles which clattered across the roof before they fell and smashed on to the terrace. He reached the edge and jumped, landing at the top of the front path, and immediately started running. I pounded after him down the path and into the *barranco*. On previous occasions I hadn't chased him any further, but today I was going to catch him. He was weaving around the drooping canes, but I followed in a straight line, my left hand in front of my face slapping the canes aside. I was wearing heavy work boots and he heard the thumping; he turned his head and our eyes met. He started to chant, 'Ai yai yai yai yai yai yai.' He was half laughing; it was just a game. I began to gain on him. He looked back and saw that I was closer. He started to chant faster, but he was no longer laughing. For 75 yards I chased him until I could reach out and touch him. I tackled him round his neck, bringing him crashing to the stony ground, and landed on top of him. I got up and he lay blubbering. I pulled back my fist - then dropped it to my side. The hatred I had felt for him evaporated. I grabbed hold of his shirt and dragged him to his feet. He was a lifeless weight and his face and hands were bleeding.

'Miguel, don't ever come to my house again. Now go home.'

He was snivelling and he wouldn't look at me. I

watched him stumble down the *barranco,* his head hanging, and I walked back to the house. All the anger had gone from me. I felt terrible. Nobody from La Venta said anything. Adela knew what had happened and she smiled at me when she saw me the next day. It was the way they would have dealt with it. The next time I encountered Miguel was when Linda and I drove past La Venta. He was standing in the *rambla* with a group of men and as soon as he saw the van he ran to a wispy sapling and, perfectly visible, crouched behind it. On other occasions when he saw me, if there was nowhere to hide, he would turn his back and stand rigid until I had gone. He never again came near the house.

CHAPTER FOURTEEN

One early morning at the beginning of April, a deputation of interested parties in the irrigation system arrived at the house. José Manzano, Paco Martin, Bernardo, and Fra'quito El Bar were there as part-owners or users; Antonio the *mulero,* together with Paco, Manolo and Antonio, the three sons of the three sisters at La Venta, were there on behalf of their fathers. They were armed with mattocks and long-handled shovels, and several wore gumboots. Antonio the *mulero* was the spokesman.

'We're going to clean the water deposit and repair the channel.'

Up to that point it hadn't occurred to me that our ten percent shareholding in the water rights would involve maintenance duties. 'Okay,' I said, 'and you want me to come and help?'

'*Claro*,' replied Antonio. 'Why else do you think we're here?'

I assumed they'd organised this a few days beforehand and I thought it would have been nice if they'd given me a bit of notice. Then it occurred to me that today was probably St Neptune or somebody's day

- the patron saint of everything to do with water. This would be the day when everyone cleaned out deposits and channels, serviced bore pumps and motors, repaired leaking pipes and faulty valves, replaced the washers on their dripping taps, and did all the other things they'd been saving up all year – and they expected me to know this. I happened to notice that the four sons who were there by proxy were the only ones wearing gumboots and carrying long-handled shovels, and that their fathers were conspicuously absent. I didn't like what that implied, so I pulled on a pair of work shoes and went off to look for my mattock.

The original syndicate of landowners had built the water deposit on the Los Morales side of the *barranco*. It irrigated fields on both sides and this had necessitated a considerable feat of engineering to construct an aqueduct across the *barranco* to supply water to the Los Sanchez side. The designers had sensibly decided not to employ the same engineering principles that the Romans had used when they constructed the multi-layered, arched aqueduct down the road at Nerja, but instead had based it more on the style of a mini Clifton Suspension Bridge. The builders first erected two massive stone piers, one on either bank, of sufficient strength to withstand the power of the *barranco* at full flood. They passed a 12 inch diameter asbestos pipe through the two piers, some ten feet above the floor of the *barranco*. The problem was, when the pipe filled with water, it became extremely heavy and had to be supported. The builders overcame this by installing a metal collar at the mid-way point of the pipe and from this they stretched a number of heavy-gauge wires to the tops of the two piers. They then tensioned the wires by twisting them together with the use of a tourniquet. It was ingenious and effective and, more to the point, it had cost very little to build - and I was hugely impressed.

The work party split up into three groups. Bernardo, Paco Martin and Fra'quito El Bar headed upstream to clean and repair the earth channel between the deposit and the point where the *barranco* had been diverted. Antonio paired me with José to work on the 400 yard section of earth channel from the aqueduct to our house, while he and the three cousins took on the formidable task of cleaning out the deposit. The night before, Antonio had released the water into the *barranco* and all that remained in the bottom of the deposit was 12 inches of silt that had accumulated during the past year. The deposit was 25 feet long, 12 feet wide and 6 feet deep, and the only way to clean it was to climb in and shovel the silt out. I watched for a few minutes as the four men heaved shovel-loads of sloppy mud above their heads and over the sides of the deposit. I now understood why the sons were deputising for their fathers and I was feeling really pleased that I'd opted for the mattock and a pair of shoes.

Close to the aqueduct, the channel was overgrown with clumps of brambles and gorse, and a nearby stand of canes had spread and was trespassing. For the next 200 yards the channel clung to the side of a hill, where earth and rock falls had caused partial blockages; in other places the outer edge had eroded and was in danger of collapsing. The channel then disappeared into a clay pipe under the mule path, before emerging alongside our house. The water still flowed along the channel, but slowly and inefficiently, losing much to seepage and periodically overflowed onto the land. Our task was to hack away the encroaching vegetation and then dig out and repair the channel. I set to work with a vengeance, the mattock high above my head, employing massive, flamboyant swings that smashed aside all in their path, each blow a contender for a fairground coconut.

José studied me for a few moments and then made downward pushing movements with his hand. *'Poco, poco, hombre - tranquilo.'*

'Tranquilo nada. Come on, José, let's get on with it or we'll be here all day.'

José started forty yards away and we worked towards each other. He used short, unhurried strokes, with minimal back-lift, and developed a steady rhythm, while I continued to bludgeon the landscape, intent on reaching the halfway point before him. When I got there, he was still five yards away and I leant on my mattock and grinned at him. Over the following forty yards, José was only a few strokes away from me when I stopped. I didn't grin this time and I noticed that he had the trace of a smile. During the next forty yards, my swings became flabby, my back hurt, and I badly wanted to sit down, but José kept up his monotonous pace and, with a sinking feeling, I realized he could do this all day. That time he narrowly beat me. I had not learned my lesson from Bernardo when I was planting the potatoes, and there followed the classic case of the tortoise and the hare. I was trounced by a man 35 years my senior, who didn't stop at the halfway point but carried on each time until he reached me. By the end, it was complete humiliation; my mattock no longer cut through the soil and roots; instead it bounced back and attacked my ankles, and I was barely doing ten yards to his thirty.

I had to sit down. *'Tranquilo, José. Poco, poco, hombre.* What's all the hurry?'

José laughed, took out his cigarettes, and sat down beside me. 'It's almost time to stop, anyway.'

José had reintroduced me to smoking. I hadn't had a cigarette for more than five years, but here all the men smoked and, one day when José offered me a cigarette, I accepted. After that, almost without noticing, I slipped into the habit. The dark tobacco had a seductive perfume that was as much a part of Spain as *paella* and *sangria*. The smell was in every bar in every plaza and on every street in every town, and it impregnated the men's clothing and their breath. José smoked a brand of cigarettes called Celtas, which were made from tobacco grown in Andalucía and cost only a few pesetas a packet. As well as being the cheapest cigarettes around, they were also the crudest. The tobacco was coarse and almost black and, when you examined it, you found it contained pieces of twig and stalk, and unidentifiable hard lumps that were presumably something to do with the tobacco plant. The tobacco was very loosely packed and on windy days the cigarettes burnt so furiously that you worked hard to get four or five puffs before they scorched your fingers. On still days they spluttered briefly before going out and you went through half a box of matches for each cigarette. I learnt to hold the cigarettes with great care because, if they were not kept completely horizontal, there was a high risk that all the tobacco would slide out of the paper. Until I became an expert at smoking Celtas, I regularly leapt to my feet with a heap of smouldering tobacco in my lap and, on one memorable occasion, I was talking to José and waving an empty cylinder of paper around while the tobacco burnt a hole in the top of my shoe. My flirtation with Celtas was brief. After a few months, I developed José's cough and spoke with a James Cagney rasp - and I stopped.

We finished our cigarettes without setting fire to the hillside and by this time it was ten o'clock. It was the time when, without fail, the workers in the fields produce the food they have brought with them wrapped inside large knotted handkerchiefs - chunks of bread and roughly cut *serrano* ham, goat's cheese, *chorizo* and olives - and often a litre of wine in a goatskin *porrón*. Work stops.

José waited while I went back to the house for food. Linda had made me sandwiches and packed them in a plastic lunch box. I tipped them out, wrapped them in a tea towel and rejoined José. We walked together up the *barranco* to the water deposit, where Antonio and the three cousins, Manolo, Antonio and Paco, were sitting on the wall, with their legs dangling over the side, above the section they had not yet cleaned. The tops of the other walls were thick with mud. There had been accidents. As a result of an ill-directed heave by one of the cousins, the back of Antonio's head and shirt

172

were caked with drying mud. I recalled the straw
episode six months before and wished I'd been there to
see it. Manolo had slipped and, from the waist down,
was a brown slick. All four had blobs of mud on their
faces, hands and arms, but they were cheerful, despite
their condition. Antonio passing round a goatskin
porrón of wine might have had something to do with it.

Brown, silty water was seeping out of the mud in
the uncleaned section and had covered the base of the
deposit in the cleaned section to a depth of several
inches. I was watching a number of frogs hopping and
splashing about, trying to get to grips with their new
environment, when I noticed that a large frog was not
conforming to the normal method of locomotion. It
appeared to be in difficulty and was moving backwards
and downwards, like a swimmer caught in an
undertow. It kicked strongly and made forward
progress for a short distance, before it was again pulled
back. I looked closely and saw that the frog's left hind
leg was entirely inside the mouth of a small snake. In
near zero visibility, the snake must have spotted the leg
and grabbed it, without realising that it was attached to
something much larger. I had read that snakes unhinge
their jaws and eat prey of greater diameter than they
are, but even allowing for this, there was no possibility
that the snake could swallow this frog, not with its right
hind leg hanging out of the side of the snake's mouth. It
needed to eat the frog head first, but to do this it would
have to let go of the left leg and then, of course, the frog
would escape. The frog wasn't strong enough to shake
off the snake, and the snake was understandably
reluctant to let go of the equivalent of a seven-course

banquet. I could see that the only way out of this impasse was when one or the other drowned. I pointed out the unfolding drama to José.

'It's a grass snake,' he said, 'and not poisonous. Don't worry.'

'I was thinking more of the frog.'

Antonio summed up the situation and reached across me for a handful of mud. He moulded it to the size of a golf ball and threw it, striking the snake just below its head. The snake disappeared beneath the surface and seconds later emerged at the far end of the deposit, where it weaved up the vertical wall and slid over the mud at the top, into the undergrowth. The frog gave a few tentative kicks, discovered it had no serious injuries, and went off to find its friends and thrill them with its adventure.

Antonio looked satisfied and passed me his *porrón*. Drinking from a goatskin *porrón* requires accuracy, timing and coordination. I raised it to my face, tilted my head back, opened my mouth like a cavern and squeezed the *porrón* gently with both hands, squirting a purple stream of wine down the front of my shirt. For some reason, Antonio and the three cousins found this hugely amusing. At my second attempt, the jet of wine went up my nose, but some dribbled into the side of my mouth. The wine was sharp and sulphurous. It must have tasted better to the four of them than the sludge they had been sampling all morning, but not by much. José and I left them sitting on the wall, passing the *porrón,* and we strolled back to the channel.

I can't explain what had possessed me to challenge

José to a mattock-wielding competition; this was the *campesinos'* tool; they were virtually born with mattocks in their hands. Suitably chastened and every muscle whimpering, I shuffled along the channel trying to follow José's example. We finished the repairs by midday and I went home and collapsed into a chair on the terrace to await comfort and sympathy from Linda. She heard my mattock clatter to the concrete and came to the kitchen door. I closed my eyes, expecting to hear cooing noises and offers of cold drinks.

'Next time,' she said, 'wear your maroon shirt.'

José had told us of a woman in a nearby village who had hens for sale. When we went there, she was in her yard scattering grain from her apron, surrounded by chickens of all sizes, every one of them white. We told her that we wanted laying hens.

'These are perfect,' she said, 'exactly what you need.'

The chickens were tall and heavy-bodied and looked to me like table birds. They were the complete opposite of the skinny, egg-laying machines we had bought in Bristol.

'Are they for eating?' I asked.

'They are perfect for eating, exactly what you need,' she said.

'But do they lay eggs?'

She thrust her hands deep into the pocket of her apron. '*Claro.* They're chickens; of course they lay eggs.'

We bought four that were at point-of-lay and let them loose in the run. These birds were professional

175

scratchers and foragers and they immediately set to work. They systematically cleared a small area and, if one of the hens dug up a long worm, she started to cluck excitedly, causing the other three to come over. There followed an exhilarating and noisy chase until she managed to swallow the worm, or else one of the others darted in and stole it from her and became the target of the chase. It was great sport, but they'd have been terrible poker players. The hens were good natured and docile and, because they were not going to end up in the pot, became our pets. They started laying about a week after we bought them and most days we had either three or four eggs. Every night, I went down to the chicken *corral*, checked that their crops were full and locked them in. Sometimes in the summer, on warm, velvety evenings, I would sit outside with a glass of wine, resting my back against the stone wall of the *corral* and listen to them shuffle and murmur as they settled on their perches, and reflect on the events that had brought us here, to this extraordinary and wonderful place.

Several months later, we were invited to lunch at the home of newfound friends, Adrian and Barbara, an English couple who had recently bought a house near Castell and intended to live there for part of the year. Adrian was an osteopath and, as well as being good company, was a very useful person to know. Lunch continued into the evening and, by the time we arrived back home it was well after dark. I went straight to the chicken *corral* to lock the door. There was no rustling of wings or shifting on the perches, no murmuring, no grumpiness at being disturbed. I ran to the van for a torch and tore back. The floor of the *corral* was like snow, deep in feathers, but there was not one chicken inside. We followed a trail of feathers diagonally across the field down to the *barranco* and for a further fifty yards to the *rambla,* before we turned and went back. We were desolate. We'd been out eating and boozing, and had neglected our livestock. It was unforgivable. Neither of us slept and in the morning, pale and miserable, we followed the feathers for nearly a mile as they became more infrequent, until finally they stopped, not ten yards from the *corral* where José kept his goats and his dog. We searched in all directions but there were no more feathers. This was the end of the trail; José's dog had taken the chickens. If only it had been someone else's dog, but there was no other explanation. We went to see José and he came with us to examine the paper-trail of feathers. The three of us stood outside his *corral*; I thought he was going to cry. Linda put her arm around his shoulders.

'It is a terrible thing that has happened, a *desastre,*' José said. 'I will pay you for your chickens and I will destroy the dog.'

'It was just as much our fault, José,' I said. 'We left the chicken house open. We don't want you to pay us anything.' But I knew that, whatever I said, José would still pay us. It was a matter of honour and, if he had to, he would visit the lady who had sold us the chickens to find out how much they had cost us.

Later that morning José's cousin, *primo* Agosto, visited us from La Venta. He walked across the field and looked inside the chicken *corral* before he came up to the terrace. We shook hands and, without entering into the usual pleasantries, he immediately came to the purpose of his visit.

'It was *el zorro* and not José's dog that took your chickens. I saw the fox yesterday on the ridge above La Venta and early this morning my son saw it on the slopes behind José's *corral*. When a fox goes into a chicken house, it kills every one of them. It is a frenzied attack - a blood lust. Once it is over, it carries them in its mouth, one at a time, to its lair. It keeps coming back until it has them all. You are saying it was José's dog, but a dog does not do this.'

'But the feathers lead to his *corral* and stop. How do you explain that?'

'It is strange, but if it was José's dog, then where are your chickens? It could not possibly eat them all and, even if it could, there would be blood and a pile of feathers on the ground or in José's *corral*, but there is nothing.' He smiled slightly. 'It was unlucky for José, but perhaps his *corral* was the spot your chickens had no more feathers to lose. This was definitely *el zorro,* and it has taken your chickens to its lair.'

We drove with *primo* Agosto to José's house. His dog was still alive; it was its usual lean and bad-tempered self and it didn't look as though it had just eaten four chickens.

'I am sorry, José,' I said. 'The feathers ... we thought it was your dog.'

José was not angry, for the evidence had been damning. He also had believed that his dog was responsible and was immensely relieved that it wasn't. If *primo* Agosto and his son had not seen the fox, there would have been a dreadful miscarriage of justice.

'Sometimes,' said Linda, as we drove back to the house, 'this simple life in Spain gets seriously complicated.'

CHAPTER FIFTEEN

There were empty *cortijos* everywhere. The slopes and valleys were littered with their crumbling stonework. In rare instances, the houses were virtually intact - little changed from the day that the families walked out, or the last member was carried out. In other cases, almost nothing remained apart from stone footings that revealed the outline of where the buildings had once been, like the architectural dig of an ancient civilization. Whole villages had been abandoned, now taken over by pigeons, swallows and rodents, and providing temporary lodgings for the nomadic shepherds, who tramped the mountain slopes with their scrawny flocks in a never-ending search for food.

There had been only one criteria for choosing the site for a dwelling - a supply of water - a spring or a well that produced enough, all year round, to sustain life. The houses had been built long before people had cars, when transport was their legs, or a mule if they were lucky, and often the only access was a rough path that followed the contours of the land.

These isolated communities did not have electricity. There were no schools, no doctors, and the closest village that was large enough to support a shop was often half-a-day's walk. The children who were brought up there seized the first chance to leave. Times had changed; they saw a way out of the mind-destroying boredom, the tedium of tending the goats, picking and shelling almonds day after day, the endless round of chores, with bare subsistence the reward. Instead, the daughters married young and left to live in towns where they had electricity, running water and bathrooms - and then produced a succession of plump babies. The sons escaped to Cordoba or Granada and worked in the factories, bought cars and looked down on those who had stayed behind. Each year the rainfall was less; wells, springs, and once-permanent streams began to dry up and *cortijos* and entire hamlets were doomed. The people could live without gas and electricity, but not without water. The family members who had remained eventually died or were forced to leave through illness or lack of water. The few possessions of value were taken away and the houses locked up.

Some of the houses were visited each year by the family. In August, inland Andalucía is like a furnace. It is the time that families take their annual *vacación* and migrate to the coast, where it is a few degrees cooler. The old *cortijos* would be dusted out and sons and daughters would spend the vacation there with their spouses and children, and make daily pilgrimages to the beach. The women sat under their parasols while the children played in the sea and the men drank in the bars that had been set up on the beach. The returning sons and daughters were now relatively affluent and

drove around in Seats or Jeeps. They were not allowed
to come back poor and, for a month, they threw money
around like millionaires.

Carlos Risueño had opened people's eyes to the
fact that, incomprehensibly, foreigners were willing to
pay large sums of money for rural properties that had
previously been considered worthless. When the
returning families learned that we had bought Los
Sanchez, the men came to visit us. The cities had
changed them. Their gaze was calculating and they
would arrive and stand near the house, saying nothing
until I offered them a glass of wine. They replied '*Me es
igual.*'- I don't mind – but always took it. They told me
that it was fifty degrees Celsius in Cordoba and we were
living in one of the best places in Andalucía. It was
cooler, unspoilt, no pollution, the life was healthy, and
there was *mucho tranquilidad*. The irony was lost on
them that, at the earliest opportunity, they themselves
had bolted like escaping prisoners. Having given me
their sales pitch, then came the reason for their visit.
Perhaps we had rich friends who would also like to live
in this paradise, because their family just so happened
to have a *cortijo, muy precioso*, that they would sell for
a very reasonable price. They would have another glass
of wine and then take me to look at this unique
property. Linda was never invited. This was man's
business.

I would ask if it was far and their replies were the
same. 'No, no - a short walk - just over the ridge - you
can almost see it from here.' We would scramble for
hours in blazing heat on the rough mountain tracks,
while they continually reassured me that we were

nearly there. The tracks were little used and kept passable only by the occasional *mulero* who ploughed around the almond trees on the upper slopes. The mountain shrubs that were now encroaching had to survive droughts and the searing heat of summer, and repel foraging goats, sheep and wild boar. As a result, they had evolved into some of the most inhospitable plants on earth. Brambles, gorse, and wild asparagus - nature's very own razor wire - ripped at my flesh as I stumbled along. At last, parched, bleeding and beyond caring, I was told that we had arrived and I was about to be shown the bargain of the year. Their expressions were now open and honest. I had seen the same look on the face of a car salesman when he had told me that the rumbles coming from the back axle were loose tools in the boot, and had turned up the radio when I mentioned the knocking I could hear in the engine.

'No one will buy a property this remote.'

'*No problema*. You bulldoze a road. You need only to get permission from the four landowners whose properties we have crossed. I know them all personally. For a small cost they will allow you access.'

'Does the house have water?'

'Of course. From the spring that feeds the deposit.' I would be shown a deposit that had a jungle of weeds growing in it and not the slightest trace of moisture. 'The spring needs unblocking, that is all. It is a simple matter, at most a morning's work.'

'The house doesn't have electricity and it will be impossible to bring it all this way.'

They were expecting this. The solution was obvious. 'Solar power,' they would say triumphantly, as though they had invented it. 'Here in Andalucía the sun always shines. You will have unlimited electricity and it will cost you nothing.'

We knew several people who had installed solar electricity in their *cortijos*, rather than pay thousands of pounds to have a power line run several miles. They had twelve-volt systems that were little better than our early days with candles and hurricane lamps.

The property was sounding less and less appealing, and then they would casually deliver the death sentence and mention that it was jointly owned by five brothers and sisters, two of whom lived in Madrid. 'But it is easy. I will get them to come here to sign the papers. The whole matter is completely straightforward.' I knew that the reverse would be the case, the endless wrangling that would ensue, the near impossibility of getting five people to agree to the sale of their inheritance, and the tangled mess of bureaucracy if they ever did.

All the returning summer visitors had a house to sell. In their eyes, the fact that we had come to live here made us stupid, and the fact that we were able to made us rich. We were credited with the unlikely combination of wealth and stupidity, which made us ripe for the taking.

Not all the properties were completely unsuitable. During my mother's stay we were visited by Juan Romero. He grew up in the valley and had inherited two properties that he was now trying to sell. My mother still had her cottage in the south of France, but she expressed an interest in looking at houses close to

Los Sanchez. I said I thought it was pointless, when she could stay with us any time she wanted. If she came with her husband, and they felt that they were imposing or wanted privacy, they could rent one of the chalets in Castell. These were always empty apart from during July and August and no one in their right mind would want to visit then. Nevertheless, we went with Juan Romero to look at the two properties.

The first was a large farmhouse in an isolated position, with magnificent views, but it had the usual problems of access, limited water and no electricity. The second property was in Ferrer, the village where Benny had bought a house. In Andalucía, village houses evolve haphazardly into a higgledy-piggledy jumble, with kitchens leading into thoughtlessly added mule stables and terraces looking directly into neighbours' bedrooms. But this house was on the edge of the village, with a small garden and no immediate neighbours. There was very little prospect that electricity would be brought to Ferrer within the next ten years, but the house was in good condition, had adequate water from a spring, and was accessed via the tortuous earth road leading off the *rambla*. At the price Juan Romero was asking, the house was good value. It was also far enough away from Los Sanchez, and with a sufficiently poor road, that our visits to each other would be rare treats. I told my mother that I thought the house was worth considering, at which she revealed the true reason for her interest.

'Yes, it will be perfect for Paul,' she said, apparently believing it should have been obvious to me from the beginning why we were looking at houses.

Paul Esnault was my mother's oldest friend. He came from a small village in Belgium and, as a teenager during World War II, he cycled the length of German-occupied France, remarkably evading capture and imprisonment. He reached Marseilles, joined the French Foreign Legion and fought in North Africa where he contracted tuberculosis and almost died. After the war, he received a disability pension from the Belgian Government and, in recognition of his efforts, was offered citizenship of any of the allied countries. He chose England, worked as a car mechanic and married Irene. As a child, I remember our visits to their tiny council house in Bracknell. Before the end of evening, Paul would have donned a woman's wig or a battered sombrero and be acting out one of his countless adventures. The room would be full of noise, excitement, and a haze of smoke from Paul's cigars, and ring with my mother and Irene's laughter. They were alive and they brought everyone else alive. When life in Bracknell became too mundane, they would pack their children and some camping gear into an old van, cross the channel and live like gypsies, eking out Paul's pension until the approaching winter and lack of money forced them home. Broke, and desperate for his next pension cheque, Paul would look for a job. My mother sometimes lent them money but never told my father, who disapproved of their lifestyle. Paul had numerous mechanics' jobs, including a brief spell as a uniformed RAC patrolman, when he rode a motorcycle and sidecar and gave exaggerated salutes to passing motorists who had RAC badges on their cars. I thought this was very romantic and used to practise his gloved

186

salute in the mirror. In later years, Paul developed a bad back which, together with his war disability, made it harder for him to work underneath cars on cold concrete in unheated workshops. He was looking for a way out.

Like my mother, Paul and Irene turned up on our doorstep without warning. We were dozing after a late lunch, when a van drove up the *barranco*, hooting continuously. 'Someone else who thinks their horn's our doorbell,' I groaned and went down to see what they were selling. Paul and Irene stepped out from the passenger seats and I went through my, 'Oh, what a lovely surprise,' routine.

'We did write,' said Paul, 'more than a week ago.' But, unlike my mother's telegram, their letter never did arrive.

The following day, we went to look at Juan Romero's house in Ferrer and in the evening we sat around our kitchen table, with a bottle of wine, while Paul and Irene worked out their finances.

'It will be cheap to live in Ferrer,' I said. 'You won't have any water, electricity or phone bills. Food and drink aren't expensive over here, and heating costs nothing if you collect the wood and cut it yourself. Land tax will be minimal and you won't pay council rates for facilities and infrastructure, for the simple reason that there are no facilities or infrastructure.'

As my mother had predicted, the house in Ferrer was perfect. By the end of the bottle of wine, Paul had calculated that he and Irene could live like royalty on his Belgian pension and still save money, so there was really no point in working any longer. Being the expert on house purchases and having unlimited patience, Linda went with Paul and Irene the next day to see Juan Romero, and later spent days with them at government offices helping them negotiate their way around all the bureaucratic pitfalls. After seven days of intense pressure, mainly on Linda, Paul and Irene signed the contract, paid the ten per cent deposit, and departed the following day, all smiles.

Linda was exhausted. 'I hope no more of your mother's friends decide to buy down here.'

It looked as though our exalted status in the community as the only foreign residents would shortly be gone and there were further signs that we would soon be part of a growing expatriate population. As well as Carlos Risueño, other estate agents were now operating and *cortijos* and village houses were being bought all around us, mainly by the British. It was brought home to us just how imminent the British invasion was when Bernardo came over from Los Morales, told me that they were selling their house and asked me if I would help him move his wine press. For years, Carmela had been trying to persuade him to move to Castell. It was the ambition of all the local women, once their children had grown up, to leave the isolation of the *cortijos* and retire in a *pueblo*. Bernardo and Carmela had no children and their friends had either died or moved to Castell. Now, all that was left was their feud with Fra'quito and Adela. In Castell, Carmela could go to the market every day, gossip with her friends, and dress in smart clothes to promenade in the evening. Bernardo, of course, hated the idea. His life revolved around his vines, his orchard and his crops of beans. He was not yet ready to be thrown out of the house to spend all day on a bench in Castell plaza with the other old men. I had seen them there, sitting in rows, with nothing to do. They held their walking sticks upright between their closed legs, gripping the handles with both hands, watching the familiar activities, idling away the hours. The women all wanted to leave the hamlets and move to a town. The men all wanted to stay.

It had become a favourite topic of conversation, how much a foreigner had paid for a local house that everyone knew had no water and, in any event, would collapse in the next storm. Carmela had seen how much these *loco extranjerros* were paying and had persuaded Bernardo that now was the time to sell, before they all came to their senses. They put their house on the market through Carlos Risueño, but Bernardo compromised; he would not sell the two-roomed outhouse, in which he would install his wine press together with a table and chairs, and he would keep all his land apart from a small olive grove. Once the house was sold he would drive his *moto* up the *rambla* every day from Castell and go back in the evening. It would keep them both happy.

Carlos Risueño brought a succession of people to look at their house, nearly all of whom were English. Carlos was as charming and handsome as ever. We hadn't bumped into him for a while and I was pleased to see that he'd put on a bit of weight around the stomach. He told us that business was still good, but the expectations of sellers was higher and, of course, there was now the competition. He had been offered a management role with a record company in Madrid and was considering it. He told us that he had previously been in the recording business and also a member of a professional band, until he became tired of playing *La Cucaracha* and *Guantanamera* for the tourists and he had quit. I once saw him pick up a child's miniature plastic guitar, tune it for a few seconds, then strum it, thump it, stamp his feet, and produce Phil Spectre's wall of sound. There seemed to be nothing he couldn't do.

One day he arrived at Bernardo and Carmela's house accompanied by a very attractive, elegantly-dressed blonde. She looked as though she would be more at home in Marbella, and I saw her gaze around the valley as if she was puzzled why she was here. The next day she returned on her own and parked her car at the foot of Los Morales. She was wearing a tight pink skirt and stiletto heels, and for about twenty-five yards she teetered and stumbled, with flailing arms, up the steep, uneven, cobbled path that led to Bernardo and Carmela's house. We watched from our terrace, while Adela and Fra'quito craned their heads over their balcony and followed her progress with interest. She finally fell over and clambered the last forty yards on her hands and knees. Needless to say, she bought the house, which is a testament to Carlos Risueño's extraordinary powers.

After the sale went through, Bernardo carried on with his life as though nothing had changed. The only difference was he now slept in Castell. He commuted every day to Los Morales on his *moto*, arriving early in the morning and returning late in the afternoon. We regularly saw him riding up the *rambla* towards us, when we were on our way to Castell or Motril. Bernardo had the only *moto* in the area fitted with a large Perspex windshield. It was out of all proportion to his *moto* and resembled a small sail. From the front, all you could see of Bernardo was the top of his hat. After the first couple of encounters with Bernardo on his *moto,* we realised that he had a serious problem with his eyesight, or alternatively the windshield was so filthy he could see nothing through it. It was customary on the narrow tracks along the *rambla* for *motos* to give way to cars and trucks – for the simple reason that they would come off worse if they didn't. Bernardo was the exception. He kept to the middle of the track, from a distance looking like an approaching square-rigger, and did not budge, presumably on the principal that motor gives way to sail. The first time we met, I realised that I would have to pull over or else run into him, and I swung the wheel, bumped into the rough and stopped. He sailed past, his eyes downwards, fixed on the five yard section of track in front of him. We waved but he didn't recognise us. Here we were, the only two vehicles on a single vehicle track, passing within a few feet of each other, and he didn't know us. That in itself was remarkable, but when you consider that the decrepit Bedford, with no windscreen and the steering wheel on the wrong side, was arguably the most distinctive van in the whole province of Granada, let alone the *rambla,* it was truly astonishing.

The good thing about Bernardo's windshield was that it gave us plenty of warning to take evasive action.

In future, when we saw it bobbing towards us, we looked for a parallel track to turn on to, or alternatively we pulled over, stopped the van and waited until he passed. On all the occasions we did that, he did not once realise it was us and return our waves.

We were unsure how we would react when the British started to arrive in large numbers, particularly having them directly opposite us in Los Morales. Much of the pleasure of living here was that we were part of a Spanish community that was unaffected by the commercialism of the coast and had not adjusted its culture to accommodate tourism. The unspoilt, traditional character of the area would change for ever, although it would be wonderful to have people we could talk to in our own language. One of the hardest things about living in Spain was not being able to express exactly what we wanted to say. We had the thoughts of adults locked up in the vocabulary of children. Our conversations with our neighbours were about their crops, the weather, their goats and chickens, and the local gossip. To converse beyond this basic level involved head-splitting concentration and a good dictionary; and for us to understand a joke in Spanish, especially a play on words, needed boundless patience on the part of the teller.

The effect of the British invasion was already starting to show. In Castell's shops we heard English voices, north-country accents asking for two Coca Colas, not a word of Spanish apart from *gracias*, which they pronounced grassy-arse. Complete strangers, who in England would have crossed the street to avoid saying hello, came up and spoke to us like old friends. The common bond of language united us, but old habits die hard and, out of season, we would see English families at either end of an otherwise deserted bay, with a yawning expanse of sand between them. If they had been Spanish, they would have been sitting on top of each other.

Bernardo and Carmela's house remained unoccupied until the following summer, when the lady with the model looks and high heels arrived with her family. They returned our waves and then ignored us. But, of course, they were completely unaware of our status as the English pioneers, the vanguard of the invasion as it were, so we decided we'd better go over and tell them. We saw that she had adopted footwear of a type not normally seen away from the slopes of Everest and was managing to remain upright. They had bought the house purely for holidays and were likely to visit only at Easter and in the summer. The rest of the year it would be empty.

We were overjoyed.

CHAPTER SIXTEEN

Castell has two faces. For ten months of the year, until the tourists descend in July, Castell is a quiet fishing village and a small commercial centre for the surrounding rural area. Its whitewashed buildings cluster around the plaza and clamber over each other towards the crumbling lookout turret at the top of the hill. The main road between Almeria and Malaga passes through Castell, separating the beachfront from the plaza, and the relentless coastal traffic, all year round, competes with the sound of the Mediterranean. Some years before, the government approved plans for a by-pass. They started to build a four lane highway to the east of Castell, heading inland, and they constructed an impressive concrete bridge across a *rambla,* but then the works came to a halt. The piles supporting the bridge had started to subside and engineers discovered that the sub-soil was unstable. After spending millions, the project was abandoned and the bridge that goes from nowhere to nowhere was left as a monument to man's folly - a companion to the turret on the hill. So, Castell remained unfashionable, with its crippling pebbled beach, thundering traffic, and inconvenient location midway between Malaga and Almeria airports.

During the day, the fishermen's boats are winched up the pebbles beyond the high water mark and left on their sides. It is the work of six men. Men with hedgehog stubble on teak faces, who sit against the sea wall waiting for the boats to come in. Three of them man the long wooden spar that turns the winch and, straining at forty-five degrees, they heave it round, slipping and stumbling on the pebbles. Each revolution, they jump in unison over the taut wire, like girls over a skipping rope. Sweating and grunting, they curse the world in general - and each other, when one slides to his knees. The other men keep the boat steady and place logs under the bow; then run round to the stern to collect them and repeat the process as the boat creeps up the beach. These are open rowing boats, massively built from heavy timber, with a string of lights bolted to the bow to attract the fish. At night the boats are scattered across the black sea, mirroring the constellations above them. The Spanish fishermen row differently to the English. With irrefutable logic, they face the bow, in the direction they are travelling, whereas the English sit facing the stern and have to keep turning around to see where they are going.

The Mediterranean is fickle. For days it is calm; there are no hidden currents and people swim in safety. Then something happens. Towering waves crash onto Castell's beach and rearrange its contours, creating miniature cliffs and exposing coarse sand, before the sea gradually flattens the beach over the following days and again it becomes an uninterrupted layer of pebbles.

The fishermen's boats are built to survive, and after the storm they are cleaned, patched up and put back to work. Once or twice each year, the sea crosses the road and floods the plaza to a depth of nearly a foot. The water retreats, leaving sand and pebbles and driftwood littering the ground. Municipal workers clear up; shopkeepers shrug and sweep out their shops, and life continues.

On the beach there was a ramshackle restaurant that was open for most of the year. It was built on stilts and projected into the sea. The restaurant was called *Los Pescadores*, but to the English speakers it was known as the Stilton. At high tide the whole restaurant was beyond the water line and customers entered via a long ramp, like the gangplank of a ship. The walls were at odd angles and the floorboards were twisted and broken and had sections missing, through which you could see the water several feet below, sloshing about. Women only went there once wearing high heels. Linda and I visited the Stilton one Sunday for lunch and sat at a table at the far end of the restaurant, well over the water, with uninterrupted views out to sea. The day was perfect; the sun glinted on a slight swell and a cool breeze came off the water. We ordered a mixed fish platter, chips and salad, which was standard fare in the local restaurants. Just as the meal was about to be served, Linda put down her glass of wine and stopped talking. Her face had turned white and there was a greenish hue around her mouth.

'Are you unwell, *señora?*' asked the waiter.

'I know this sounds strange,' Linda said, 'but I

think I'm seasick.'

We moved to the front of the restaurant, closer to dry land, and Linda recovered enough to eat the meal. Less than four months later a storm hit Castell and the Stilton disintegrated. It was a sad loss. There are not many restaurants that can make you seasick.

There were a handful of small bars in Castell that remained open all year. They were for the men of the village - open for coffee and cognac first thing in the morning, and for wine and beer at lunchtime and in the evening, before the men went home to eat with their families. Our favourite of these bars was *El Terrible*. It was away from the plaza and the beach, in a narrow cobbled street of whitewashed buildings, and its drinks were a few pesetas cheaper. The owner was a fisherman, and his wife and daughter ran the bar. There were two tables and a few bar stools, but otherwise you stood. The bars in Castell gained their reputations from the *tapas* that they served free with the drinks and *El Terrible's* were the best. A single sardine, caught that morning, seared on a hot plate for several seconds, before being flipped over and served, sizzling, with a quarter of lemon; home made blood sausage on a corner of crusty bread; or a tiny saucer of paella. Each was exquisite and designed not to satisfy the customer's appetite, but to stimulate his thirst. One Saturday, Linda and I attempted to lunch there on beer and *tapas*, and can vouch for the fact that by late afternoon we were eventually able to fill our stomachs, but afterwards we found walking a problem.

The first time we visited *El Terrible*, we were on our way back from an unexpectedly successful

197

shopping expedition to Motril where, amongst other things, we managed to buy some plumbing fittings that had eluded us for weeks. In a happy frame of mind, we stopped in Castell and stumbled across *El Terrible*. We were enticed in by the smell of their paella. It was a little after midday and there were only a scattering of people inside. By one o'clock the room was full of men. Some were calling in for a couple of looseners before going home to their wives; others were settling in for the duration. The men looked at us briefly as they came in and then ignored us. We were squeezed to the end of the bar and the noise increased. Spaniards are incapable of talking quietly - they shout as though they are permanently angry. It appeared that an argument was in progress involving most of the bar; voices cracked like gunfire and, at any moment, I could see bar stools being thrown. One man, who could shout louder than anyone else, bellowed something and the men around him exploded with laughter. It started deep in their guts and erupted out of wide open mouths with heads thrown back. The men waved their arms around and slapped each other on the back and punched people's shoulders. There was a brief lull while spilled drinks were replaced, before the noise resumed. We saw that we had never been alive. The restrained murmur of the English pub was like the reading room of the library compared to this.

Our principal bank was in Motril, at which we carried out the majority of our transactions. However, at the small bank in Castell we had an account with a modest balance, which we kept mainly for emergencies. The bank in Castell didn't send out statements to their customers and, on our infrequent visits, we were handed wads of paper that the bank appeared to generate daily, none of which showed any alteration to our balance. The three men who worked there had a standing in the local community. For a few pesetas, their shoes were polished every morning by a boy who sat on his box at the entrance to the bank, and they arrived smelling of aftershave, with their trousers and shirts neatly pressed. Their hair was oiled and their hands were soft and clean. Many of their customers were poorly-dressed inarticulate peasants, who could not read and whose signature was a thumbprint. We watched the bank officials read out documents, fast and carelessly, to old men and women, whose faces showed not a flicker of understanding; and, when they had finished, roughly grasp their hands, jam their thumbs onto the ink pad and press them to the paper. For all they knew, they could have been signing away their homes, but these peasants placed complete trust in the officials; to them, they represented knowledge and authority. The men in the bank enjoyed their small-town importance, but when they encountered someone like Carlos Risueño it was entirely different. They deferred to him; they let him use their phones and conduct his business from their foyer.

They were not interested in tasks outside their daily routine. Once, after standing in a queue for twenty minutes, I tried to organise an overseas telegraphic transfer. The official barely looked up. 'You must go to a bank in Motril.'

Another time, I wanted to change a traveller's

cheque. 'This is not possible - try a bank in Motril.'

'Are you a bank,' I said, 'or a bread shop?'

'We are a bank, of course, *señor*. If you want to buy bread you must go to the *panaderia* around the corner.'

The other pillar of bureaucracy was the post office. The postmaster delivered letters to the residents of Castell, but otherwise the mail was kept in alphabetical order in a filing cabinet to await collection. Our mail was sent to Rubité and delivered to us by Gonzales and Son, although occasionally someone would address a letter to us at Castell and we periodically went to the post office to check. The problem was that none of the mail in the filing cabinet was ever thrown away. There was tons of it, including dozens of letters, years old, addressed to Jim and Doris Brown. I once asked who these people were, but no one knew. The other difficulty was that, although the letters were filed alphabetically, there was no consistency with the system. The letters addressed to Mr & Mrs Jim and Doris Brown were spread, fairly equally, under M, J, D and B. So, when Linda and I went there to see if we had any mail, to be on the safe side, we took half the alphabet each and looked under every letter - which is why we know all about Jim and Doris.

The tiny *mercado* was in the same building as the post office and boasted the most beautiful butcher in Spain. She had Sophia Loren looks and a personality and laugh that filled the market. At home, she had two young children and a husband who was older and said to be very serious. In the mornings, she worked behind the marble slab in the market and chopped and sold meat, but every week I expected her to be gone - discovered and whisked off to Madrid to make films - but she was happy and she stayed. The first time we went to the market, there was a group of women waiting to be served by her. She stopped what she was doing, called us over and served us ahead of them, all the time making jokes at our expense, to the amusement of the women. We understood little of what she said, but we could see there was no malice; we were just entertainment to relieve the sameness of their days. When we became regular customers she gave us presents, half a pig's lung to fry with garlic, four chickens' feet for soup, pork fat to render for lard, or a small piece of meat left over from a previous order. Each Saturday, we bought a great lump of her lowest grade pork and, as soon as we were back at the *cortijo*, spent half an hour cutting and sorting it into pieces good enough to grill, fry or roast and the rest for casseroles and stews. Our meat diet at that time was rabbit, pork and chicken. We couldn't afford beef or kid and the three or four times we bought mutton it was inedible. I am convinced that Andalucían sheep are allowed to live long and happy lives, and it is only when they eventually die of natural causes that they end up on the butcher's slab.

During the last two weeks of June everything changes. Castell becomes a hive of industry. Men who have spent the last nine months cultivating runner beans- but cannot grow them in the heat of summer - arrive with *albanils* and start to tear down the boarding and shuttering on the beach bars. The interiors are swept out and painted; electric cables criss-cross the beach and strings of lights are draped around the buildings; parasols made out of palm fronds are erected outside the bars; chairs and tables with red and white check tablecloths are set up. The farmers hone their cooking skills, try to remember how to operate the pressure kegs of beer, and practise being polite to the tourists. The season is about to begin - a brief two months in which to make money.

Castell beach, which had looked forlorn the week before, begins to fill up and towel space near the water is at a premium. The shops do a roaring trade in plastic sandals. It is the only time of the year that the mini-market has queues and the *panadería* cannot bake fast enough to meet demand. Music pumps out all day from the bars on the beach that, by late morning, are full of shouting men. Enterprising people transform their lock-up garages into boutiques selling pottery and basket work, and turn their courtyards into barbeque restaurants. Two camping grounds open at either end of the beach and have full signs within a week. Tents, which the police pretend not to see, appear in out-of-the-way spots. Night clubs that have gathered dust for ten months are hosed down and, with kaleidoscope lighting, are made to look attractive enough to justify the outrageous prices of the drinks, and people with enviable stamina gyrate until five in the morning to Queen and Dire Straits.

For one week in July it is the fiesta of Castell. It starts with a procession in which a full-size statue of the Virgin Mary is carried out of the church and borne solemnly around the streets on strong shoulders. After she is safely back inside, the fiesta begins in earnest. A fairground company sets up its equipment between the beach and the road, and after dark Castell comes alive, with crowds thronging the beachfront and the plaza. The music from the big dipper competes with the packed beach bars and, as the chairs go higher and spin faster, the music accelerates, and shrieks and occasional flecks of vomit drift down from the sky, and young children fight over coins that fall to the ground. Girls wearing white blouses and short, tight skirts strut about with trays of soft apples covered with teeth-breaking caramel; and stallholders selling hot donuts and pink candy floss with remarkable adhesive qualities, cajole passers-by. Grizzled men, who are normally seen going high into the mountains armed with shotguns to hunt wild boar, exchange their weapons for air rifles and use their skill to knock back the teeth of clowns - and take home fluffy toys. In the plaza, a group of schoolgirls, resplendent in satin flamenco costumes, with ribbons and brightly-coloured combs in their hair, posture before a table of solemn judges and a crowd of clapping women. They dance with set faces and haughty flicks of the head, with raised arms and feet that move like tappets. The winners receive rosettes the size of lettuces.

Paco, Manolo and Antonio, the sons of the three sisters in La Venta, come into Castell in the early evening to try their luck - Paco, intelligent and dependable - Manolo, with his film star looks and terrible stammer - and Antonio, serious and kind. Freshly shaven, hair combed and wearing their best clothes, they are hardly recognisable. They stand in a tongue-tied group around the girls. They could have told them how to prune olive trees, the best time to plant runner beans, and about the delicate technique of bud grafting, but what could they say that would entertain these smart girls from Cordoba and Granada? Besides, the moment they spoke with their funny accents they would reveal themselves.

Then, at the end of August, it stops. The Spanish holidaymakers return to the cities and their jobs. Overnight, the bars close and the shutters reappear. The foreign tourists, with nothing left to stay for, move on; and Paco, Manolo and Antonio go back to their fields and prepare them for autumn planting.

CHAPTER SEVENTEEN

Our friends who had promised to visit us as soon as we had civilised the *cortijo* began to arrive in late spring. We had explained to everyone that we had bought a very old, primitive farmhouse which was in a run down state, and that it was in the middle of a peasant community, several miles from the Mediterranean. But, to some of our friends, after we wrote and told them that the renovations were progressing steadily, the farmhouse became transformed. It was now a villa set in formal gardens, complete with aesthetic arches, a swimming pool, and probably the odd servant or two. Not only that, the farmhouse had been transported to the fleshpots of Marbella and they were likely to step outside and rub shoulders with minor film stars. When they came they were disappointed, and two lots of visitors stayed for only a few days before heading off to Torremolinos.

Gillian and Pam, two very well-spoken ladies from Linda's painting group in Bristol, visited us out of season, when there were no tourist bars or restaurants open or, in fact, any other forms of entertainment. I felt certain that the bars in Castell, which in those days were populated entirely by unshaven, shouting men, would not appeal to two genteel ladies, and I was unsure how they would respond to our rural lifestyle. I wondered what on earth we were going to do with them for a week and was apprehensive.

Gillian and Pam had a marvellous time. Every day they went with Linda to find a different spot to paint. It was all new to them and they were prolific. There were drying paintings everywhere - whitewashed villages, landscapes of the surrounding mountains and valleys, our neighbours working in their fields, and the fishermen and their boats on Castell beach. I barely needed to leave the house to know what was going on around us. In the evenings we drank red wine and played bridge. Linda had learned to play while we were in Bristol, disliked the game, and participated only to keep the rest of us happy. Initially, Linda and I were partners and, on our second night of misunderstandings, during which I was becoming increasingly irritable, I got up to visit the bathroom. While I was gone, Linda commented that it was the first time that evening she knew what I had in my hand and what I was going to do with it. They were still laughing when I came back. After that, I partnered Gillian and the games were more peaceful.

A few months before Gillian and Pam arrived, we were given two young rabbits. For generations, the local families had bred rabbits for eating, but recent outbreaks of myxomatosis had decimated both the wild and domestic populations and, now, few people kept them. We had asked everyone we knew where we could

buy a breeding pair, without success, and it seemed
that our preparations in Bristol had been for nothing.
About two months after we had stopped asking, the
sixteen year old son of a couple in La Venta, Paco
Farina and Inocencia, came to the house carrying an
oval, finely-woven reed basket, with a close-fitting lid
and carry handle. The basket was exquisitely made and
had involved countless hours of work. Paco junior lifted
the lid and inside were two white rabbits that must
have been cousins of Winnie and Ralph. He said
nothing and held the basket out to us.

'They are wonderful,' Linda said. 'Thank you. How
much do we owe you?'

'*Nada*. They are a gift.' He was at pains to show us
that they were a buck and a doe and we were not to eat
them. Once he had done this, he was anxious to leave.
He refused the return of the basket, which his father
had made specially to carry their gift.

We hardly knew Paco and Inocencia; our
encounters with them had been limited to a few polite
buenos dias or a wave as we drove past La Venta.
Nonetheless, they had remembered that, months
before, we had wanted to buy rabbits. They could have
sold them to us for easily the equivalent of half a day's
wage, but instead they gave them to us, with little
prospect of receiving anything in return. We were
shown this unexpected generosity many times in
Andalucía, by people who had so little wealth. It was in
their character that if you asked for something they
would happily give it to you, but if you attempted to
take the same thing by trickery, you would make an
enemy for life.

We kept the rabbits in a stone *corral* beneath the terrace. Like the attic room, all the *corrals* had been built with low ceilings, fine for chickens, goats or rabbits but without thought for their minders. I knew that we would have to separate them soon and I decided to build a cage for the doe and let the buck have the run of the *corral*. A week later I was stacking wood in the adjoining store when the buck's head popped up from between two logs. It had not occurred to me that the earth and stone floor of their *corral* was perfect for burrowing. So, like Winnie and Ralph, they were both kept in cages.

One morning, while Gillian and Pam were visiting, the doe gave birth to her first litter. We about to take our guests to the market in Motril and I checked the rabbit *corral* on the way down to the van. Eight hairless pink rabbits, each about half the size of my little finger, were scattered around the floor of the doe's cage. She had made a half-hearted attempt to build a nest out of fur pulled from her stomach and small pieces of hay, but the young were nowhere close to it. I picked one of them up. It was cold and, I believed, dead. I cupped it in my hand and after a moment I felt it stir.

'Linda! Quickly - go back to the house and heat up some water.'

While Linda heated the water I ran down to the garden and rubbed parsley over my hands. Even if we could keep the litter alive, the doe was likely to reject them because of our scent and I knew that parsley would mask the smell. For the next hour we worked to save the rabbits. We filled a hot water bottle with warm water and covered it with an old woollen jumper in which we wrapped the litter. Linda cut the finger off a rubber glove and pricked the end with a pin. I heated goat's milk to body temperature and laced it with a splash of cognac. I held one of the tiny rabbits and eased open its mouth as Linda squeezed in a few drops of the milk. The effect was immediate. The rabbit's heart started pounding and its legs were kicking as if it were racing around on a tandem. I thought perhaps the cognac had been a bad idea, but after a few seconds its heart stopped thumping and its legs slowed to a leisurely trot. We treated the rest of the litter with identical results and after half an hour they felt warm enough to return to the cage. I carried them down to the *corral* and gently placed them in the nest that the doe had built, adding more hay for insulation. The doe came over and sniffed them. She looked at us as though she couldn't understand what all the fuss was about and started to rearrange her litter. I knew that as soon as we left they would start suckling.

'It won't taste as good without the cognac,' I warned them.

A few months after we arrived we heard English voices in the general store in Castell. It turned out to be a grey-haired man in his sixties with a woman in her late twenties. They had heard Linda and I talking and nodded without speaking. We returned their nods and assumed they were those inferior beings - tourists. They had thought the same about us and it wasn't until we bumped into them again several weeks later that we struck up a conversation. Nick and Janet had bought, through Carlos Risueño, a *cortijo* near Los Carlos. They were living here permanently, renovating their house and, like us, doing all the work themselves.

'Nick is not my father,' Janet said, so that there would be no misunderstanding. 'He is my partner.'

I nearly asked if she meant business partner, but thought better of it. Janet was intelligent, attractive and vivacious, and I could see why people would jump to the wrong conclusion.

'And in case you are wondering,' she added, 'I'm the one with the money.'

We laughed. We liked her already. The following weekend we paid a visit to their *cortijo*. We arrived with a bottle of wine and spent a happy few hours swapping renovation-disaster stories and admiring their building works. Their standard of workmanship was excellent. They were good at carpentry and their doors and widows fitted without our usual gaps; they built their walls straight using things like plumb lines and spirit levels. They did proper plumbing with copper pipes and Yorkshire joints - not with lengths of hosepipe and screw clips, as I did - and their bathroom had matching fittings and colour-coordinated tiles on the floor and walls. Their favourite tools were hand planes and fretsaws, whereas mine were bricklayers' trowels and hammers - the bigger the better.

They had met when they worked together in a London borough planning department, which must have shaped the way they approached these tasks. I was reluctant to invite them to look at my amateurish works, but when we got on to the subject of building a septic tank, which they had yet to do, I found that I was the expert. Not only did I know the theory, but I had built one and it actually worked. I started to feel a bit better and mentally thanked Benny. We were all missing English-speaking company and we quickly became friends. Janet had an endless supply of jokes, which I imagine they used to tell each other in the planning department to fill in the days. She told them with a wonderful style, like a teacher addressing the bottom grade in primary school. This is one of her jokes:

"On a lovely summer day, three sisters were in their parent's swimming pool. They were playing very nicely, with no pushing or splashing, and they were taking it in turns to go on the water slide. A passing angel noticed the three sisters and decided to reward them for being so well behaved. She quickly changed into a one-piece costume - backless, of course, so that her wings were free - and she landed with only the hint of a ripple in the shallow end.

'Because you have been such good girls,' said the angel, 'I am going to grant you each a wish. You must go to the top of the slide and think of your favourite drink. As you go down the slide, call out its name and I will change the water in the pool into that drink.'

Sally, the eldest, went first. She was crazy about Pepsi and, as she went down the slide, she yelled out, 'Pepsi!' When she hit the water, it magically changed into Pepsi and she drank it all up.

Jennifer, the middle sister, went next. She just loved lemonade and, as she zoomed down the slide, she screamed out, 'Lemonade!' Once again, the water magically changed to lemonade and she drank it all up.

Little Dorothy went last. She loved all fizzy drinks,

211

but her special favourite was orange Fanta. She was almost beside herself with excitement - you can just imagine. She ran up the steps to the top of the slide, almost slipping off in her rush, and she launched herself down it. But little Dorothy had become so excited she had completely forgotten what she was going to say and, as she hurtled down, she shrieked out, 'Weeeeeee!'"

Late one evening, Nick and Janet were sitting in their lounge when there was a knock at the door. Janet went to answer it and shouted out as three young men from Castell pushed past her into the lounge. They went for Nick and he reacted with remarkable speed. He jumped up, grabbed a heavy poker from the fireplace and started beating them with it. A sixty-five-year-old man proved to be a much tougher proposition than they had anticipated. He rained blows on them and under his attack they retreated to the door. He managed to force them outside, slam the door and ram home the bolt.

Nick and Janet's *cortijo* was in an isolated position at the end of a rough track. There were no neighbours within 500 yards and they had no telephone. They could hear the men talking outside and then something crashed against the front door. A few seconds later it was repeated. Nick and Janet dragged the sideboard over and wedged it against the door. They went to the back door and barricaded it with a heavy table. Their windows were fitted with external bars and they had already closed and bolted the shutters. The men tried to ram open the doors and, when that failed, they attempted to force the bars from the windows and threw rocks at the shutters. Nick and Janet spent the night under siege and, when it started to get light, the men left. After they were sure that they had gone, Nick and Janet went outside to inspect their house. The doors, shutters and walls were extensively damaged and the men had smashed their car with rocks.

The incident was so shocking and horrific, and so untypical of that peaceful region that it was difficult to believe it had occurred. Why had the three men gone to their house? Janet recognised two of them; they had been friendly to her in Castell. I had heard joking talk among the Spaniards that they thought Janet could do a lot better than Nick and that she would appreciate the attentions of a young and virile bull, in fact someone just like themselves. Was this what they had in mind? Had they gone there to tie Nick up and rape Janet - and then what were they going to do? She could identify them. At their trial they said that their motive was robbery. I don't believe it. You don't burgle the house of people who know you, not while they are in it. They were found guilty and given the choice of serving their sentence in prison or in the Spanish military, the conditions of which were apparently similar. They chose the military.

Nick and Janet sold their *cortijo* and went to live on an urbanisation near Almería, two hour's drive away. We went to see them. They were happy. Their house was small with a tiny garden, and surrounded by similar houses. It was safe, but little different to living on an estate in England, except the sun shone. They were too far away to visit regularly. We missed their company; we missed their laughter and their friendship; and we especially missed Janet's jokes which, incidentally, are best served with wine.

The summer brought an influx of the British who had bought properties to use as holiday homes. The first couple we met were Pat and Ronnie - the parents of Benny's wife – whose public-school accents seemed strangely out of place in Castell plaza. They were instantly friendly and invited us to their house that evening for drinks. They owned a large *cortijo* that had access via a track leading off the *rambla,* about halfway between Los Sanchez and Castell. Their house had no electricity and the large expense of bringing it from the *rambla,* for a property used for only a few months of the year, was not worthwhile. Instead, they had installed 12 volt solar power, which gave them romantic lighting in all rooms, but little else.

We arrived on the Ossa at six-thirty and Pat and Ronnie welcomed us effusively. Ronnie made four gin and tonics that were mainly gin - tonic was nearly as expensive as gin at that time in Spain and nowhere near as much fun – and we carried our drinks with us as they showed us around their *cortijo* and told us about themselves. Pat and Ronnie made their money from Tupperware. They held senior positions in the organisation and controlled a number of teams that consisted of regional supervisors who, in turn, controlled area representatives. The infrastructure went all the way down to newly married housewives, who held parties at which the Tupperware representatives sold their friends plastic containers with lifetime guarantees and lids that fitted properly. In return, the housewives received a gift of one of those round, compartmentalised plastic dishes designed to hold peanuts, olives and cocktail onions, and cubes of cheese and pineapple impaled on toothpicks – and which would come in very handy at their next Tupperware party.

Their *cortijo* had large, cool rooms with expensive furnishings, grand arches leading to paved courtyards and vine-covered terraces, and a swimming pool. It was in an elevated position with superb views of Castell and the Mediterranean and they owned most of the surrounding hillsides, which were planted with hundreds of almond trees. They had arranged for a local man to look after them and harvest the crop. I stood with Ronnie on the main terrace, admired the view, and told him that I thought their property was magnificent.

'You're right, dear boy,' he said, 'but I'm not sure I'm happy coming here every year for our holidays.' He gestured at the sea of plastic greenhouses that lined the *rambla*. 'Every time I catch a glimpse of that lot, it straightaway reminds me of work.'

They were amusing, attentive, charming hosts and we had a fabulous evening. They drank copious amounts and did it in a hurry. As they drank, their humour became sharper and, as the evening progressed, there emerged an undercurrent. The banter between them developed an edge and their jokes were now barbed. Linda looked at me and I nodded. It was late and it was time to leave. We said goodbye at the front door and they were as delightful and charming as ever, but we had not reached the bike when we heard a plate smash and raised public-school voices using language I had not heard since my scaffolding days.

The Ossa was going through one of its good phases, but I was wishing we hadn't brought it. We had to negotiate the steep, twisting earth road from their house, and then we had the *rambla* to contend with. Late at night there were never any other vehicles to bump into and we were now familiar with all the criss-crossing paths that seduced people into the hills, but the *rambla* was full of holes and rocks and ridges. I hadn't counted the number of gin and tonics Ronnie had poured me, but the way I was feeling I would have been much happier on four wheels. We made it home safely, but I vowed that the next time we visited them we would take the Bedford.

Throughout the summer, Pat and Ronnie's extensive entourage presented itself. Their two sons, younger daughter and assorted close family, and their respective spouses, partners and friends - and friends of their friends - arrived in stages. We socialised with them all and it was great fun, but they were here on holiday for just a few weeks for the sole purpose of partying and although we tried valiantly we couldn't keep up with them either financially or physically.

CHAPTER EIGHTEEN

The first winter, we were unprepared for the cold. We wore layer after layer, but still we froze. This was southern Spain and it shouldn't be like this. The lounge, with the only fireplace in the house, still had an earth floor and huge sections of plaster missing from the walls and, when it rained, water seeped through the back wall and ran across the floor. It was months away from being habitable. So, we wintered in the kitchen, huddled around a foul-smelling paraffin heater, and watched its thin coil of smoke collect between the rafters and blacken the low ceiling. When the wind was from the north, smelling of snow, it channelled down the *rambla,* all the way from Don Quixote's La Mancha, over the peaks of the sierras, and pierced like his lance. It forced its way around our crude-fitting doors and through every gap in every shutter. Inside the kitchen door, our flock-lined curtain, its bottom hem weighted with stones, billowed like a spinnaker.

The second year we started our preparations early. During our walks we collected fallen branches and logs and, sweating, dragged them back and piled them in the field. By late October we had a mountain of wood,

217

worthy of the largest Guy Fawkes' bonfire, and we laboured with a bow saw to cut it into lengths that fitted the fireplace.

José watched our efforts with amusement. 'You are truly getting full value from your wood,' he said. 'It makes you warm three times your way, but only once when you need it and twice when you don't.'

He was soon to start on his own, very different, preparations for winter heating, and he declared, one afternoon, that he was about to make charcoal. I had never thought much about charcoal before. It had always been in the form of thin, messy sticks that they had given us at primary school to produce smudgy and unrecognisable sketches. It had never occurred to me that it was a serious form of fuel.

The following morning, José announced his arrival with his customary, sheep-like cough, as he emerged from behind the fig tree at the bottom of the path. 'Today,' he said, 'I am starting the *carbón*.'

He launched into a discussion with himself about the weather over the forthcoming two weeks and continued this monologue, uninterrupted, for several minutes. José had the ability to talk about the weather for longer than anyone I have ever known, but this was extraordinary, even for him, and it wasn't until he had finished that the reason was revealed. The process for making charcoal needed consistency of weather. This was vital; otherwise it would be a disaster. He told me that first he had to dig the pit, and I could assist him with this as it did not require a large degree of skill. So, for the next hour, we toiled over a grave-sized pit in La Marina's field on the other side of the *barranco*, directly opposite our bedroom window.

'From now on,' said José, 'the process is *complicado*, so you will not be able to help me, but you may watch.'

José had selected prunings from the almond trees that covered the nearby hillsides and these were laid out on the ground alongside the freshly dug pit. With short, accurate chops from a small hatchet, he removed the side shoots, until he had uniform bundles of finger-diameter sticks. I offered to help, but José had witnessed my attempts to cut canes with a blunt axe and he feared there would be other digit-sized objects in the pit, if he allowed me to use his razor-sharp hatchet.

He placed dry grass and kindling in the bottom of the pit and, afterwards, the bundles of trimmed almond prunings, bound with wire. He constructed a roof from sticks and grass and then shovelled on top some of the earth we had dug out. At one end he had left a small opening, into which he dropped a lighted piece of paper. He checked to make sure the kindling was alight and then blocked it up.

'The combustion process is very delicate,' said José, 'and requires the precise amount of air to enter the pit. The combustion must be very slow because, if it is too fast ...' He raised clenched hands and opened them both quickly. 'Poof ... the *carbón* will have disappeared and all that is left is ash. Ash,' he repeated, 'no good for anything but sprinkling on the land. And, if there is not enough air, the fire will go out.' His face turned solemn as he contemplated this tragedy. 'To light it again is almost impossible, and my work will

219

have been for nothing. So, if the wind gets stronger, I will add earth to the roof, exactly the right amount to the gram, in order to maintain the rate of combustion, and when the wind dies I will remove it. The fire needs extreme vigilance and must be monitored twenty-four hours a day. The young of today do not possess the skill or the patience.'

For two days the weather remained calm and José's visits to the pit needed nothing more than adding or removing a few handfuls of earth, which, I am sure, was done solely for my benefit. On the third night it all changed. At eleven–thirty I lay in bed and listened to the low moan of the wind and the rattle of the shutters. After half an hour, huge spots of rain were drumming on the roof and the wind was howling around the house, blasting its way under the tiles and bringing down clouds of whitewash from the ceilings. I wondered if José, true to his word, would walk a mile up the *rambla* to shovel earth on top of the pit, and not just randomly, but measured to the gram. I decided to get up and watch from the window.

José did not own a raincoat and when he was forced to go out in the rain he wore a plastic fertiliser bag that had holes cut out for his head and arms. In exceptional conditions, he adopted full wet-weather gear. He had cut a bag diagonally across a bottom corner and wore it like a crude sou' wester on top of his cap. He additionally wrapped fertiliser bags around his arms and legs, and tied them in place with black nylon cord, but he did this only in dire circumstances, because they rustled and squeaked as he moved and severely restricted his mobility.

After a few minutes I saw the dim glow of a swinging lantern. In the intermittent light, as clouds raced across the moon, and from the occasional flash of lightning, I watched José's stiff-legged approach. He looked like a badly-dressed lifeboat man. As he came nearer to the house, I pulled back into the darkest corner of the room. When he drew level, he jerked his left arm up in a half-wave. He could not possibly have seen me, but somehow he knew I would be watching.

The following morning, when the wind had blown itself out, José came back and shovelled away the earth that he had piled on to the roof of the pit during the storm. Afterwards, he walked over to the house.

'*Hombre,*' he said, 'last night, during the *tormenta,* I thought you would have come over to help me.'

'*Tormenta?*' I said. 'What *tormenta?* I must have slept right through it.'

José looked at me and smiled.

After about twelve days, the charcoal was done to José's satisfaction and he doused the smouldering pit with water. When he removed the charcoal, it filled three fertiliser bags and seemed a paltry reward for the work required to produce it.

'It will last the winter,' said José. 'You use very little; I will show you one day when it is cold. Now, the pit must be filled. It would be dangerous to leave it open; goats or sheep could fall in.'

I knew that his main concern for the diminutive, itinerant shepherd, known as *Cebollito* - Little Onion - who slept rough, on a straw mattress, in a room at the rear of Los Morales. Little Onion had come down from the Sierra Nevada, with his small flock of

221

sheep, and would take them back in the spring after the snow cleared. He went to the bar in Los Carlos every night and spent his money on *vino costa*. Several times, I had heard him singing hoarsely as he stumbled back in the dark and, one morning, I had found him asleep at the bottom of our path.

'Yes,' repeated José, 'we must fill in the pit.'

'Are you sure I have the skills to help you?' I asked.

'I believe so, yes,' said José. 'After all, it is only shovelling.'

We first encountered charcoal in operation, not at José's home, but at Francisco *Alcalde* and Madelena's. We called at their house to return an axe that I had borrowed and Madelena invited us in. Francisco and their children, Paco and Mari-Carmen, were seated around the table in the kitchen. Every home in the area had an identical round, wooden table, with four legs set slightly in from its perimeter; between the legs, approximately six inches from the ground, was a flat board with a circular hole, about the size of a large dinner plate, in its centre. We had thought that the board was for people to rest their feet on and the hole purely ornamental, but now we saw its real purpose. There was a metal dish of glowing charcoal resting in the hole and the family had been toasting its feet. It seemed an unusual way to heat a house and I said so. While Francisco fetched a bottle of wine, Madelena showed us how it worked. She brought out an enormous round tablecloth which, when she spread it over the table, went right to the floor. She told us to sit down and adjust the cloth around our legs in order to trap the hot air inside the table. The result of this, of course, is that anyone sitting at the table roasts from the waist down, while their upper parts remain unheated. Strangely, though, the system seemed to work and Linda and I soon developed a cosy all-over glow – although I have a feeling the wine probably contributed to this.

After half an hour, Madalena got up from the table and checked her pot of stew. She sat down again and sniffed the air and said something to Francisco. He opened the back door, went outside, and returned shaking his head. Almost immediately, Linda let out a yelp and jumped up from the table, stamping her left foot. The sole of her tennis shoe was on fire. Francisco acted quickly. He grabbed a bucket of water from alongside the sink – I can only assume he kept it there for this purpose - and poured it over Linda's foot. She kicked off her shoe and it lay on the kitchen floor, hissing and steaming, and giving off an unpleasant odour of smouldering Dunlop. While Madelena clucked around Linda, Francisco went off to refill the bucket – presumably in case Linda decided to set fire to her other shoe - and Paco, Mari-Carmen and I sat at the table and enjoyed the moment.

The metal dish of glowing charcoal was the only form of heating for most homes in the area. Although it was unquestionably clean, cheap and efficient, it had one insurmountable flaw - it was effective only while you were glued to the kitchen table. The moment you got up it was entirely useless. Also, accidents were commonplace and we now understood the significance of the charred skeletons of tables that people tossed

from their balconies into the *rambla*. We decided not
to adopt the traditional heating method, but instead
had large, blazing, often smoky, and very uneconomical
log fires.

CHAPTER NINETEEN

Paul and Irene arrived with their daughter, Giselle, almost a year to the day after we came to live at Los Sanchez. They had paid for the house in Ferrer, settled their affairs in England, packed as many of their possessions as they could into an old van, and were here for good. Paul had officially retired. A month before they arrived, Cristobal and his wife, Mari-Carmen, bought a house in Ferrer and moved in. Cristobal was returning to the area that he had left many years before to make his fortune. He had ended up working as a cleaner in Barcelona where he met Mari-Carmen. They saved enough money to buy the house, a flock of sheep and a Land-Rover. Cristobal was happy to be back, but Mari-Carmen was a city girl and hated the primitive living conditions and isolation of Ferrer. She was one of the few women in the area who drove, and she spent a lot of her time socialising in Castell while Cristobal walked his sheep on the slopes. She was delighted when Paul and Irene arrived and, for the first time in more than a decade, Ferrer had a resident population of five.

Through Paul and Irene, we became friendly with

Cristobal and Mari-Carmen. We invited the four of them for lunch one Sunday and spent the morning preparing the meal. We were using ingredients from our land, which dictated the menu. For the entrée, we made beetroot soup, and for the main course a rabbit casserole with onions, beans and potatoes. It was too cold and windy to eat on the terrace and we laid the table in the lounge. Linda brought out the bowls of soup and embarked on a story about the time we made it for a dinner party in Bristol when, for no apparent reason, it turned out an unpleasant shade of brown and, in desperation, we added curry powder and tried to convince everyone it was mulligatawny. Halfway through the story, Cristobal lowered his head until it was level with his bowl and took his first spoonful of soup. He sounded as though he was pulling a corpse out of a swamp. It arrested Linda in mid sentence and Irene paused with her spoon an inch from her mouth. Paul and I looked at each other and grinned, but Mari-Carmen appeared to be oblivious. Cristobal had another mouthful and made exactly the same noise. I did what any host would have done and slurped my soup companionably. Paul caught my eye, winked, and made a noise like someone plunging a sink. Linda covered her mouth with her serviette and Irene excused herself from the table while Paul and I spent the next few minutes trying to outdo each other and Cristobal in a soup-slurping, lip-smacking extravaganza.

A few weeks later, one evening towards the end of January, we were visiting Paul and Irene in Ferrer. Cristobal and Mari-Carmen were there and we were coming to the end of a long and enjoyable meal -

although, to my disappointment, Irene had not served soup. Paul, Cristobal and I were savouring one of Paul's better brandies and the women were trying to come to terms with a bottle of home-made Irish Cream that I had brought round. My mother had sent me a recipe from Libya that she had spent some time experimenting with and, according to her, had now perfected. Libya is a dry country and the only booze that was readily available was whisky, which was smuggled in by the pilots. My mother didn't like whisky and had been trying to find a way to make it palatable. The recipe was 50% whisky, a couple of spoonfuls of cocoa powder and the remainder approximately equal amounts of strong black coffee and cream, for which I had substituted José's goats' milk. I was explaining to them that it was an acquired taste and improved the more of it they drank, when there was a knock on the front door. The room jumped as one.

I must explain the unlikelihood of this occurring. It was ten o'clock at night, in the middle of winter, in the middle of nowhere, in an up-until-recently abandoned village on top of a hill, accessed by kilometres of horseshoe bends on a steep, rutted earth road. The entire population of Ferrer was collected together in Paul and Irene's house, which was situated one hundred yards further on from the village along a rough track. There were no lights in the village to help a person thread their way through the empty streets. In daylight, the house was hard to find. Without a map, in the dark, it was almost impossible.

Paul took a hurricane lamp from the table and went to answer the door. He came back to the dining

227

room and stood in the doorway. 'Are you expecting guests?'

'Guests?' said Linda, 'No, I don't think so.'

'Well, anyway, they've arrived.'

Friends from Western Australia, Jean and Peter, whom we had not seen for five years, were doing a backpacking tour of Europe, with their two children, Joseph and Rachel. They had found themselves in Granada and decided to pay us a visit, travelling by public transport. The coach ride from Granada to Castell had been straightforward, but from there it had become difficult. Their Spanish was non-existent and no one they had asked in Castell had heard of Los Sanchez. Los Morales was part of our postal address, but in Castell it was more commonly, although incorrectly, known as Los Morarillos - which is the same name as another hamlet in the next valley. Consequently, they were given varying directions. The only taxi operator in Castell refused to drive his new car onto the *ramblas* to check out the two hamlets and it wasn't until Peter started throwing money at him that he agreed to borrow an old Citroen 2CV van and help them find our house. When they finally arrived at the correct Los Morales, it was late into the evening. The driver established from Adela that we lived opposite at Los Sanchez, but we had gone out on the motorbike. She didn't know where, although it was possible that we were visiting the other *extranjeros* in Ferrer. When she gave the driver directions, he blanched and said he could not possibly take his friend's car up a mountain at night. To a couple who had brought two young children backpacking around Europe and, not only that, had left the warmth of the Australian summer to come to the European winter, this represented a minor challenge. They were now close and Jean was not going to be denied.

'Offer him some more money,' she said to Peter, 'a lot more.'

The driver allowed himself to be persuaded and, after following a few wrong tracks, they were eventually on what they hoped was the Ferrer road. The 2CV was carrying five people and four backpacks. At the first steep horseshoe bend it stalled in first gear and rolled backwards. The four passengers got out and pushed the 2CV round the bend. They got back in and it did exactly the same at the next one. After the third bend they didn't bother getting back in and ended up pushing the Citroen most of the way to Ferrer. They arrived at an unlit, completely deserted village full of partly derelict buildings and narrow cobbled streets. They shouted our names, knocked on doors and stumbled around in the dark. They hadn't eaten; they were cold and tired; and they almost reached the point of telling the driver to take them back to Castell and they would try again in the morning. The only reason they found us was that Jean glimpsed a momentary square of light when I went outside to the toilet. At first she thought she had imagined it, but a short while later she saw the light again. It was the only time I have ever been thankful for a cactus-patch lavatory.

We did all the tourist things. We combed the beach at Castell and had prizes for anyone who found a rare piece of red or yellow glass worn smooth like a gemstone, or a matching pair of flip flops or plastic beach shoes; we took them to our spring where the water comes out of the rock and, without being told, Joseph casually walked over and pulled out the bung; I roared around on the Ossa with Joseph hanging on behind me and Rachel between my arms, perched on top of the petrol tank. We walked up the *rambla* and had a picnic at Paradise Found, a deserted hamlet with a lagoon full of water and two date palms alongside, all the buildings still intact, their shutters rattling in the breeze. What had made the people leave and where had they gone? José let the children try to milk his goats and they had the same lack of success as Linda and I. In the evenings we played games. Charades was the children's favourite and we split into two teams. Joseph mimed pop songs that had not yet arrived in Andalucía. For Queen's *Another One Bites the Dust,* he lay face down, chewing at the floor, while Linda and I looked on, perplexed. Eventually, he got up and, in disgust, went through the words syllable by syllable.

They stayed with us for five days. It was not long enough. On their last day we took them to Haza de Lino for the famous kid casserole. It was a cool, sunny morning when we set off from Los Sanchez. By the time we reached Rubité there was a layer of muddy cloud and a few flakes of snow were drifting in the air. For most of the year, snow sits on the higher peaks of the Sierra Nevada, but we were at only 2,500 feet and it was the first time we had seen snow at this altitude. For Joseph and Rachel it was the first time they had *ever* seen snow. As we climbed higher to the ridge, the snow thickened. Peter and I were in the front. We put fertiliser bags over our sheepskin coats; the snow landed against them, melted, and ran down onto our trousers. For the first time in nearly eighteen months I turned on the windscreen wipers. To my delight, they worked, dancing about a few inches from our noses, while Peter and I pretended to use them to clear our glasses.

I stopped the van at the T-junction with the ridge. We climbed out and looked back the way we had come, where the road to Rubité writhed below us, black and glistening. We crossed the road and the Sierra Nevada was spread out before us. The whole range down to the lower slopes was covered in snow. The twin giants, Pico de Veleta and Mulhacén - the highest mountain in mainland Spain - soared to more than 11,000 feet. In some lights at certain times of the year, the mountains are dull-grey, sombre and brooding, but that day they were pure Walt Disney magic.

When we arrived at the restaurant it was still snowing, although it was not settling. We sat close to the log fire and had a fabulous meal. Twice, I left the table to check outside. The second time there was a covering of snow on the road; the sky was darker and the air was thick with large flakes. I went back inside. 'I think we should hurry up and finish the meal.'

It was three o'clock when we came out of the restaurant. The roof of the van was covered with snow and there was three inches lying on the road. It was snowing heavily. Joseph and Rachel pelted each other and Jean with snowballs while Peter and Linda looked on and laughed, and I looked on and worried. Years before, on our way back to England from Spain, Linda

231

and I visited Andorra to buy duty-free drink. It started snowing while we were in the shops and we ended up trapped there for seven days, snowed in. Every day we attempted to drive out and each time we were forced to turn round and go back down to the township. On one attempt we slid backwards, handbrake on, terrified and helpless, until the vehicle ploughed into a snowdrift on the inside of the road. If the vehicle had drifted to the outside, we would have gone over the edge.

I pictured the road back to Los Sanchez. We would be fairly safe as we drove along the ridge - it was undulating with a few curves - but, when we turned off to Rubité, the road dropped more than 1,000 feet in a few miles. Apart from being incredibly steep in places, the road was single vehicle width, continual hairpin bends, and had no guard rails. I decided it would be suicidal to go back the way we had come. If we kept following the road past Haza de Lino, in the opposite direction to Rubité, it was a gradual descent to the coast, east of Castell. There were a few bends, but it was two lanes all the way and, to the best of my recollection, most of the sections had guard rails. It was about four times as far, but we stood a better chance of getting home alive.

I took Peter and Linda to one side and told them. We were all originally from England and we had grown up with snow, but not on roads like these. Peter shrugged. 'It doesn't matter to us. You live here; you know what the roads are like. You do what you think is best.'

I let air out of the tyres while the snowball fight raged around me. Peter and Linda had teamed up with

Jean, and Rachel and Joseph were now using the van as a shield. Cunningly, the three adults effected a pincer movement and, outnumbered and outmanoeuvred, the children were being peppered. The snow had eased and the temperature was dropping. It would not melt now until the morning. I threw a snowball and hit Peter on the back.

'Snow good,' I said, 'we've got to get going.'

We left the car park with them singing, 'Snow business like snow business.'

At the restaurant, I had drunk two glasses of wine and Peter had asked me if I was unwell. What little I did drink left me the moment we were on the road. The snow was unbroken by vehicle tracks; the houses opposite were shuttered and smoke was coming from their chimneys. No one would move now until tomorrow. The Bedford's steering felt light; I coaxed it round the first curve, stopped and let more air out of the tyres. I drove hunched over the wheel, easing the van down the mountain, with the muscles across my neck and shoulders forming into a knot. At every bend I remembered Gonzo's bread van and I imagined six frozen lumps being found, days later, buried in the snow. For more than an hour we crawled the descent and during the whole time we saw only one other vehicle, a car fishtailing towards us at speed up a long steady hill, shooting snow from its back wheels. The boot was up and, as we passed, we saw three grinning men sitting in it, facing backwards with their legs hanging over the bumper, bouncing up and down as they tried to make the wheels grip. I watched the men in my wing mirror. They were completely unconcerned

233

as they waved and called out to us. The children laughed and returned their waves through the back window.

As we came closer to the coast, the snow gradually turned to slush and finally to wet road and we all cheered. For no logical reason, Jean started to sing *Ten Green Bottles* and everyone raucously joined in. For a brief moment, I almost wished we were back on the snow. I let out a long breath, sat back in my seat, and the muscles in my neck and shoulders began to loosen. We reached sea level at La Rabita and drove along the coast road to Castell and up the *rambla* to Los Sanchez - the completion of a huge circle. The sky was blue and the sun had dipped below the ridge. I asked Adela if it had snowed. She just laughed.

Early the next morning we drove them into Castell to catch the coach back to Granada. We mooched around the house. We were both thinking how wonderful it had been to have the children around. We didn't need to say anything to each other; we had decided to have children of our own.

CHAPTER TWENTY

Not one of the Spaniards we knew from our locality played sport. Part of the reason was that they led physically hard lives and had little excess energy, but also it had never been in their culture to play sport - for generations, there had been no time or money for anything other than subsistence. But now, even if they had wanted to, there were almost no facilities. There was no golf course or basketball court; there were no swimming pools open to the public - only for the tourists at the hotels. No one cycled for pleasure; the *rambla* was terrible for cycling and the nearest tarmac road was at Castell. The only people you saw on bikes were those too poor to afford a *moto*. The single tennis court at Castell had a surface covered with leaves, a sagging, rotten net and a permanently locked gate. I once climbed the fence and discovered that the winding mechanism for the net was inoperable and players would break their ankles in the craters in the bitumen – the court hadn't been used for decades. None of the local people fished from the beach or off the rocks at Castell - although the summer visitors came loaded down with fishing rods, spear guns and nets. They also came with kayaks, ski-boats, scuba-diving gear and all manner of aquatic sporting equipment, but no one I knew locally even went for a swim regularly.

There was no major football team in the area to generate an interest in the game, although there was a football pitch of sorts in the *rambla*, close to Los Carlos. It had no grass, just dusty grey soil interspersed with rocks and pebbles and the occasional shrub. The only time I saw it used was at the fiesta of Los Carlos when the village side took on a team of All-comers. Players drifted on and off the pitch during the game and I counted, at one stage - although it was hard to be sure as neither side wore matching colours - fifteen players for Los Carlos and eight for the All-comers. None of the men had football boots and several of the less committed played with drinks in their hands. Understandably, no one wanted to fall over on the stony ground and, as a consequence, the tackling was lacklustre. Despite this, players regularly took a huge swing at the ball, missed it altogether, and tumbled over in the process. The players with drinks refused to risk spilling them by heading the ball, and passes consistently went to the opposition - partly because in the melee around the ball it was difficult to tell whose side anyone was on and also because, regardless of who had the ball, players on both sides called out for it.

The shortest person on the pitch was in goal for Los Carlos. He spent the game leaning against one of the posts, smoking and drinking beer. His main role was to let off three rockets whenever Los Carlos scored. There was little difference in the level of skill or application of either team but, as a result of their inferior numbers, most of the play was in the All-comers' half and Los Carlos's goals were frequent. Every time they scored, their goalkeeper pushed himself off the post, put down his beer, and pulled a rocket out of an open box. He held the firework in his right hand, transferred the cigarette from his mouth to the touch paper, and loosely pointed the rocket in the direction of the All-comers' goal. If it had exploded, it would have blown off his hand. When fire and sparks poured out of the rocket, he let go and it flew with a trail of pink smoke, in a low trajectory, the length of the pitch. The players were expecting it and leapt out of the way if it came towards them. He let off a further two rockets and then resumed his position against the post. Once, I saw him shoot a rocket between the goalposts at the other end, with the All-comers' goalkeeper having dived for cover. To the general hilarity of spectators and players, Los Carlos was awarded a bonus goal. This match could in no way be confused with Real Madrid playing Barcelona.

In the cities and large towns, you saw old men, with arms and legs missing, selling lottery tickets. I had always assumed that they were veterans of the civil war but, after having watched Los Carlos versus the All-comers, I now thought it was more likely they were firework victims.

In the evenings, in the towns and villages throughout Andalucía, people go out on to the streets for the ritual of the promenade - *el paseo*. It is, to a large extent, a substitute for sport and contains a number of its key elements. The *paseo* involves exercise in the fresh air -

albeit in the form of an unhurried stroll punctuated with frequent stops. There is regular interaction with the other participants; if you encounter a neighbour, someone you have not seen since early morning, the excitement is intense, the adrenalin rush the equivalent of scoring a goal. There is a fierce element of competition. Appearance is critical. To *pasear* in work clothes would be unthinkable. The elderly wear formal clothes – suits and dresses and jackets, and hats and bone-handled canes - that echo of long-past eras. But their splayed and bunioned feet let them down and they shuffle along in carpet slippers. For the young girls, clothes, hair and makeup are paramount. The days of girls being allowed out only if they are chaperoned are long gone. It is important to look good; it is more important to be seen looking good; and it is even better to be seen looking good with someone really cool hanging off your arm. The young men tend not to walk - unless they are with a girl - but congregate in small groups at strategic points along the route and make comments at the passing girls, who pretend that they aren't there. The girls avoid any eye contact, but see everything with heightened peripheral vision. They maintain their composure for ten paces before giggling for the next fifty.

In Castell there was a fixed route to *pasear*. You started in the plaza, crossed the main road on to the beach-front path and continued for three quarters of a mile until the path stopped near the camping ground. You then turned round and walked back the same way. In summer, the route was lined with temporary bars, and tourists and locals thronged and jostled. The outside lane, against the sea wall, was highly prized, with locals refusing to give way to tourists coming from the opposite direction. It would have been logical to walk somewhere less crowded, but the promenaders were equally participants and spectators, where the object was to see and be seen. To have walked, free from jostling, through the backstreets of Castell where you met nobody, would have been pointless.

In July and August the diversions increased. You saw what the chic girls from Granada and Cordoba were wearing - fashions that had not yet appeared in the shops in Motril, and when they finally did arrive the chic girls would be wearing something different. The foreigners provided a fresh source of entertainment. Castell was not a destination for fashionable young singles - they went to places like Marbella and Puerto Banus - but couples and families stopped for a few days en route to somewhere else. The newly-arrived English had skin so translucently white it was almost blue, and it was patterned with pink stripes and patches where they had missed with the sunscreen. The men wore baggy shorts and heavy sandals with beige socks – and, hilariously, the English always apologised when the locals muscled them away from the sea wall. There were large German women who sunbathed topless all day on the beach - to the delight of the local fishermen - and now displayed yards of broiled cleavage glistening with après sol, and red, chunky legs that ballooned out of tiny shorts. Their husbands wore short-sleeved shirts, completely unbuttoned, revealing bristle-haired guts of staggering proportions.

This was entertainment of the highest quality.

The people in the *cortijos* and hamlets didn't promenade. There were no fashion parades up and down the *rambla*. The *campesinos* walked miles every day through necessity; what possible reason could they have for strolling about without purpose in the evening, dressed in their best clothes? The same logic governed their lives. Every plant they grew had a function. It either produced something to eat or to sell, or provided shade or building materials. The only exception was the profusion of geraniums around the houses, but these were planted where little else would grow. Few animals were kept as pets. There was not enough money to feed an unproductive mouth. Cats lived in the *corrals* and kept down the rats and mice; dogs rounded up sheep and guarded the animals, or flushed out game during the hunting season.

Shooting was the men's only diversion. Once a year, at the time of the Los Carlos fiesta, a clay-pigeon competition was held in the *rambla* against the backdrop of the red clay cliffs near La Venta. It attracted the best shots from the locality and the level of skill was high. It was taken seriously and there were no goatskin *porróns* in evidence. Other than the expletives after every miss, there was little talking and the camaraderie between men who customarily worked side by side in the fields was absent. This competition was for the experts. For the average shooter, whose gun reposed under his bed for most of the year, there was always a pressing engagement that prevented him from entering the clay-pigeon competition, and it was the *caza* - the hunting season - when he brought out his armoury. At the start of the season, men carrying double-barrelled shotguns and wearing two bandoliers of cartridges - enough to destroy every wild boar in the valley - collected in groups of four or five with their dogs. Hunters set off on their *motos* and went into the mountains. They took with them, strapped to the rear racks, caged partridges to sing and entice a mate, which was destined not to live long enough to consummate the relationship. Under the guise of sport, the men hid in the undergrowth, guns cocked, and blew the amorous partridges to pieces, taking care not to shoot their own birds. For a sport, it was singularly unsporting. We watched two of these hunters riding side by side up the Rubité road; their guns slung across their shoulders, the barrels pointing towards each other like accusing fingers.

The massacre was brief. For a week, battles raged around us and bird-shot hailed down on the roof. We left the house and spent the days in Motril. The boars went deep into the dense vegetation in the gullies, and the surviving partridges flew off and kept flying, or else spent the days hiding in Castell plaza, masquerading as town pigeons, hoping they wouldn't be spotted. The men tired of going out at dawn and returning with nothing - and it ended.

Our neighbours' lives seemed to consist of long hours of hard and tedious work. They made no distinction between weekdays and weekends and, when they had any spare time, their leisure activities were productive. They sat together on their terraces; the men wove split-canes and reeds into baskets, or panniers for the mules,

241

while the women crocheted bedspreads and tablecloths. Televisions were not yet common in people's homes and no one read. Most families did not own a car; the men rode *motos* to the fields where they worked. When their wives rode with them to go to the market at Castell, they sat side-saddle on the pillion with a wicker shopping basket across their knees, resting one hand on their husband's shoulders. The *motos* were too slow to drive all the way to Motril; they left them in Castell and took the bus. Families did not go away on holiday - they were tied to their homes by their animals and their crops, but also where would they go? They had the sea and the mountains on their doorstep. They spoke no other language and what would be the point of going to another part of Spain? It was bad enough when they had to go into Motril. They had no desire to see different places and many of the people in the valley had not travelled further from their homes than Malaga or Granada, two hours' drive away. We were used to being entertained at cinemas or theatres, eating out in restaurants and going abroad for our holidays, but their money was too hard-earned to fritter away on such trivial things. Frugality was ingrained in their souls. Any money that was left over, after paying for the necessities, was saved. It would go towards another parcel of land or a piece of farm machinery.

Their lives appeared to be largely unchanging - dictated only by the seasons. But things *were* changing. On the coast road between Castell and Adra was a restaurant called *Los Amigos*. We had stopped there several times for reviving glasses of wine, on the way back from spending fruitless mornings at the *notario's* office in Adra, trying to sort out the deeds for our house. On those occasions there had been a few men in the bar and one or two families of tourists in the restaurant. When we went there for lunch one Sunday, with a couple visiting from England, it was completely different. We arrived early and sat at our table with drinks and watched the other diners arrive. We discovered that *Los Amigos* had become the in place for a new breed of local Spanish - the ones who were making money and were prepared to spend it. We knew many of them by sight and several nodded to us as they came in. They had come down from the hamlets and *cortijos* in the hills, and from the nearby coastal villages. Men - who we were used to seeing dressed in nylon trousers, cotton check shirts, and sandals made from car tyres, their uncombed hair stuffed under caps and pincushion stubble on their faces - arrived freshly-shaven and smelling of cologne, hair greased and plastered to their heads, looking self-consciously trendy in their new clothes. Girls and women - who rarely dressed up – entered like mannequins. The women wore no makeup when they worked in the fields; they dressed in flat canvas shoes, skirts and blouses faded by the sun, with scarves covering their hair. Today they were transformed. Newly-washed hair, shiny and black as night, flowed like manes; exuberant, henna-dyed curls were piled impossibly high, shored up by brightly-coloured combs; ringlets coiled down like serpents and rested on bare shoulders; old women's hair, still dark, was permed into tight springs. The women had applied foundation as if it was render. Mascara-blackened eyes flashed and vermillion lips smiled. Slim girls flounced past in dresses with tight bodices. Matronly hips and majestic bosoms were restrained and squeezed into exotic costumes. Red nail polish and heavy rings adorned rough hands. Women, unused to high heels, tottered to their tables and kicked them off the moment they sat down.

The level of noise was, by Spanish standards, subdued. The restaurant had started to fill and we decided it was time to order. The owner was working full-time delivering bottles of wine and the young waitress who was there when we arrived had now disappeared. Linda and I waved our hands and caught the owner's eye. He nodded and continued distributing bottles. When every table had at least one bottle of wine, he came over. There was no menu. He held his pencil poised above his notebook and gabbled a list of four or five dishes. By this time, the noise had increased; bottles were being banged on tables and conversations were taking place between people at either end of the room. He repeated the list and Linda and I made out *calamares* and fish. He was not going to say it a third time and we ordered something and hoped we wouldn't end up with four dishes of everything, which had happened on a disastrous occasion at another restaurant. As far as we could make out, it was a fixed price menu; the only variable depended on how much we drank. Our friends, who hadn't understood a word and assumed that we knew what we were doing, were paying the bill. I surreptitiously checked the contents of my wallet.

The noise had reached the level of a pop concert. Everyone was yelling - there was no other way to be heard. It had a cumulative effect. The louder people shouted, the louder everyone else had to shout. I could see that the only way it would stop was when the roof fell in. If I had taken off my shoe and banged it on the table no one would have noticed. The waitress reappeared and, with unerring judgement, dispensed bottles of wine, unasked, throughout the restaurant. The owner dumped a dish of black olives submerged in oil, and a plate of crusty bread on our table. A bottle of wine later, he returned with a mountain of salad, a quarter-litre of olive oil and a lemon. Finally, he arrived with the main course. Our friends had asked us what we'd ordered and we had told them it was a surprise - the chef's choice. It turned out to be a selection of fried whole fish and *calamare* rings, with slow-cooked, soft potato wedges that smelt of olive oil. It was simply-prepared and tasted fabulous - and, best of all, we were given just one meal each.

After three hours, our heads were ringing and we were partially deaf. The face of the man at the next table was red and glistening with sweat, and by running his hands through his hair he had made it stand up in spikes. He was yelling into the face of his wife, who was trying to lip read. Two combs had fallen from her hair and were on the table; a third was hanging trapped near her left shoulder. The henna coils had collapsed and sagged damply across her face. Her mascara had run in short rivulets and her lipstick had somehow managed to spread round to her ear. The top of their table looked as though they had been involved in a food fight. I gazed around the room; every table was the same; everyone looked exhausted. I turned back to our table and realised we were no different. It had been a remarkable meal.

CHAPTER TWENTY-ONE

José had his 65th birthday and became entitled to the government's newly-introduced pension. He was wealthier than he had ever been when he was working and, to celebrate, he had a room added on to the side of his two-roomed house in La Venta. He dressed in his best clothes, brought out a wooden chair and sat in the shade, watching and puffing on his *Celtas* while the *albanil* and his labourer worked. I called in to see how the *obras* were progressing and discovered that the extension was being built with breeze blocks, milled rafters and a corrugated asbestos roof. José, who I had believed was a traditionalist, who had helped me trim the canes for our ceilings and locate the tiles for our roof, who had shown me how to sieve and mix the mud for the stone walls, and had devoted days to making a few sacks of charcoal, was building his extension with hideous modern materials. It was inconceivable. I couldn't help myself; I harangued him.

José looked amused. '*Hombre,* you have to move with the times. Besides, it is much cheaper like this. They would take five weeks to build it the old way out of stones and mud, using canes from the *barranco* and beams from the white cedar - and the roof tiles are expensive. This way, they will be finished in a week.' His eyes twinkled. 'Now I am a pensioner I have to think of these things. Anyway, it will be my neighbours who look at it - I will be inside.'

José was going to keep his goats and would continue to work La Marina's *campo* opposite us, which he enjoyed doing, but he would stop the casual labouring that he did for landowners in the area. He would not miss walking for hours into the mountains, with a bundle of almond saplings and as much water as he could carry, chipping holes in the rock-hard ground. I once asked him what percentage of the saplings survived.

'*Depende*. If the owner has luck and it rains, and the goats and the boars don't eat them, possibly half.' It was better than I thought. I wouldn't have expected any of them to live.

José told me that he would not be making charcoal again. It was too much work and not that expensive in the shops. He had made it because he did not have the money to buy it, but now he had the money there was no point. I remembered my brother's comments about our home-made soap. Perhaps he was right after all.

Like José, we too were slowing down. By the start of our second summer we had finished the renovations. The house was moderately comfortable; we had installed a second bathroom complete with a primitive solar shower; we were producing a good supply of vegetables; we now had more than thirty rabbits and were giving them away; our Spanish was good enough to cope with most situations; and we had an increasing circle of Spanish and expatriate friends. Working in the *campo* was not a full time occupation, particularly during the summer months when little grew, and without the house renovations to keep us busy, we were both suffering the occasional twinge of aimlessness. However, on the positive side, our inactivity provided us with the perfect opportunity to socialise.

We had become good friends with Francisco *Alcalde's* daughter, Mari-Carmen, and her boyfriend, Paco, and through them we met her cousin, also named Mari-Carmen, and her husband Manolo, who were both teachers in Granada. We saw them when they made their fortnightly visits to her widower father, who lived in a *cortijo* close to Los Carlos. Manolo was from Granada and was out of place in this rural environment. He was looking for some diversion during his visits, and Linda and I provided it. He was a sporting *fanatico*. He didn't discriminate; he watched everything that came on television - from bullfighting to athletics, from football to motor racing. He was overweight and had bad knees, but was the only person I ever saw running for pleasure in the *rambla*. He persuaded me to come with him once. It was ankle-breaking terrain and I now knew why his knees were bad. He only ever had cold showers, believing that they were somehow beneficial, and was an enthusiastic but hopeless tennis player. He loved talking and would discuss anything. He had a fast brain and we had to be careful if we made asides in English. He didn't know the words, but was sharp enough to pick up the meaning. He told jokes that we rarely got first time, and he always knew when we hadn't and went over them again and again until we understood. It was the same if he was making a point in an argument. If we couldn't understand him he would try ten different ways of explaining it. It was important to him that we understood. He was different from the local people, but we didn't realise just how different until one afternoon when we returned to Los Sanchez after a trip to Castell.

Adela stopped us in the *barranco*. 'Two foreigners came to see you,' she said, 'a man and a woman.'

Our next lot of visitors weren't due for another week and I asked Adela if they had told her their names.

'No, but they were about your age and the *hombre* had curly hair and glasses. He was tall and *grande*.' She held her hands apart, level with her waist. 'He asked me if I knew where you had gone. I said I thought you had gone into the *pueblo*.'

'And the woman?'

'She had long hair, but I couldn't see anything else. She sat in their car - a white car.'

It sounded like Manolo and Mari-Carmen. 'Are you sure he was a foreigner and not Spanish?'

'He was definitely a foreigner - although he spoke quite good Spanish.'

But, of course, it was Manolo who had spoken to Adela - Manolo, who had lived all of his life in Granada, fifty miles away.

We had not met many young Spaniards from the cities. The locals had little interest in matters outside their daily lives, but Manolo was inquisitive about everything. He wanted to know about life in England and Australia. How much did we earn? Were things more expensive there? What was the weather like in Australia; was it as hot as here? What sport did they play? He knew about cricket; it was an English version of baseball. He would not accept that Australia is larger than Spain. He thought it was a small island. I had to bring out our atlas before he believed me. He was a Bob Marley fan and played his cassettes when he came round; he could quote Cervantes and Lorca, or argue with me all night about football or how Spain's middle-distance runners were better than Coe and Ovett. Gibraltar was a sore point with him.

'Why are you English occupying a part of Spain? You have no right to be here. It is Spanish sovereign land.'

'No it isn't. Spain ceded it to Britain.'

'You forced us to do that. We did not do it voluntarily. Besides, it was hundreds of years ago. Now, everyone wants Gibraltar to return to Spain.'

'The people who live there don't.'

Manolo snorted. 'What has it got to do with them? This is a question of sovereignty.'

'Well, if you don't believe that Britain has a right to remain in Gibraltar, how do you justify Spain being in Ceuta and Melilla?'

He bristled. 'That is different. Ceuta and Melilla are much closer to Spain than Gibraltar is to England.'

'Closer they may be, but they're not even in Europe.'

'That is unimportant. Anyway, we are talking about Gibraltar, not anywhere else.'

And so the argument would continue, going nowhere, but more stimulating than talking about goats and runner beans. He made me realise just how much I had missed people like him.

An ever-increasing number of English were buying properties in the region. A few had moved here permanently; others were alternating between their homes in England and Spain; but most were using their properties solely for holidays during the summer. These were people with a great deal of spare time, which largely seemed to be taken up by long meals accompanied by unusual amounts of alcohol. That summer, we slipped comfortably into their social scene and, despite all our lofty ideals, we became idle socialites.

Several of the English who had purchased properties in the area were distinctly eccentric and stamped their personalities on the region. An English woman in a nearby village bought a lamb from a local shepherd and kept it in her garden. The lamb was aesthetically pleasing and additionally fulfilled a useful function by munching the grass and weeds. Linda and I walked past the house one day and the lamb looked very fetching with its fluffy white coat and a red bow around its neck. But lambs don't stay lambs for long and their coats don't remain pristine either - they become a grubby and unattractive grey. Sheep also smell, particularly when they are not shorn. It would have been logical for the woman to have given the sheep back to the shepherd in exchange for another lamb, but by this time she had become fond of it - she had bottle-fed it when it was young and now it followed her around the garden - a faithful, if not particularly stimulating, companion. She didn't want to get rid of it but she really couldn't have this pungent and aesthetically unpleasing animal roaming the garden and attaching itself to her whenever she went outside. She overcame the problem by dyeing the sheep pink and giving it a weekly shampoo. I don't know what the sheep thought about her solution, but it caused considerable mirth among the locals.

A refined older lady bought a *cortijo* close to Castell and moved in. We were told that she was vaguely connected to Pat and Ronnie. Very soon after she arrived she decided that it was far too much trouble to learn Spanish and instead it would be easier, and probably quicker, to teach every Spaniard she came into contact with how to speak English. We heard stories of Spaniards who had spent excruciating afternoons at her house, politely partaking of tea and biscuits while they listened to her speak English. They left carrying a collection of cards with child-like drawings and words such as cat, dog and house written on the back. Spaniards started to take long detours to avoid going near her *cortijo*.

Because she was a newcomer to the area, Paul decided to pay her a visit. Despite having lived in England for more than 30 years, Paul spoke English with a strong Belgian accent, which had become more pronounced since he arrived in Spain and was speaking English less. We bumped into him the following day in the *rambla*.

'She's completely barmy,' said Paul. 'Mad as a hatter. She even tried to teach *me* how to speak English, but at least she didn't give me any of her cards.'

'That's a pity,' Linda said, 'If we collect enough of them we could rub out the names and play pairs.'

The nearby village of Gualchos was arty. It was populated by painters, sculptors and potters, and people who just dressed as though they were. It had a good proportion of foreign residents, several of whom we knew casually. One summer evening Linda and I rode there on the Ossa to eat at the outdoor restaurant near the plaza. We saw a couple we had met before and shared their table. We got on well, drank too much, and they offered to put us up for the night. The following morning I woke up parched, with a mild hangover, and meandered into the kitchen, to be met with the back view of our hostess. She was standing naked, cutting up oranges.

It was an awkward situation. If I tried to sneak back to the bedroom and she heard me, she would think I'd been spying on her. The alternative was to announce my presence with a breezy, 'Good morning' and pretend it was all quite normal. As I hovered and debated the issue, I couldn't help looking at her. She had heavy, well-muscled legs and solid buttocks, a broad waist and wide shoulders - she was not fat, just big, and every inch was tanned a uniform golden-brown. I made a decision and coughed quietly, a watered down version of José's. She stopped cutting oranges and turned round unhurriedly. I gave her what I hoped was a reassuring smile and raised my right hand level with my shoulder, palm outwards and fingers upright and slightly apart, in the universal gesture of peace; although, thinking about it, it probably looked as though I was trying to stop traffic.

'I'm sorry to disturb you; I just came for a drink.'

'That's all right. Excuse the dress, won't you? Oranges are so messy. Anyway I don't bother much with clothes in summer.' She held out a glass of juice. 'I was doing these for breakfast.'

I inched towards her and took it from her hand, all the time thinking that this is the moment Linda will walk in.

A few weeks later, we invited them for a meal and games evening at our house. Paul and Irene were there, as well as two friends, Eve and Michael, who were visiting us from England. After the meal we played charades - husbands against wives. Regardless of the mix of the teams, the games are always cutthroat, but men against women introduces an extra edge. The rules we played were that each team wrote on a slip of paper the name of a book, song, film or famous person etc. and the slip was then given to a member of the opposing team. There was a limit of ten minutes for each charade and no props or talking were allowed.

Play progressed with the usual sniping and snide remarks from both sides and after an hour the women were forging ahead. Linda, Irene and our hostess from Gualchos were giving energetic performances on the floor and Eve, who'd drunk a lot less than anyone else, was guessing everything. Something had to be done - this required drastic measures. I went to the kitchen for a bottle of my Irish Cream, poured half into a decanter, topped it up with whisky, and gave them each a glass.

It was my turn to do the charade. Linda handed

me a slip of paper with *How Green Was My Valley* written on it. That should be easy. I stood up in front of my team. They looked at me soggily, but we started off well and, within a couple of minutes, they'd guessed *How Green Was My* ... Surely they'd heard of the book and I didn't need to mime the last word - but they hadn't. I tried shaping my hands like a V. Then I mimed a river running though a steep-sided valley. All the while they sat looking at me with puzzled expressions, saying nothing. I couldn't believe they hadn't got *Valley*; it was so simple. I was tempted to do something daring involving tasteful gestures in the direction of the lady from Gualchos's cleavage, but I knew the women would disqualify me for using props - and probably lock me outside as well. I decided to do a "sounds like" and touched my ear. All I could think of was a slave galley. I manned the oars; I rowed like a man possessed; I strode up and down with a whip and I thrashed the hapless oarsmen - and I swear that each time I did that I caught a flash of amber in the eyes of the lady from Gualchos.

Finally, Michael called out, 'Slave gallery.'

I clasped my hands together and moved them from side to side - the sign for "almost right".

'Of course,' said Paul, 'a gallery.'

No, no, not a gallery – a *galley*. I implored them with facial gestures; I got on my knees and beseeched them. But, at that stage of the evening, it was all they could come up with. They believed that gallery was the correct word. I decided to go through the alphabet until I reached the letter V - then they'd get it.

'Remember what word you've got,' I said.

'No talking or you're disqualified,' said Linda.

'But I'm not telling them anything. I just want to make sure they haven't forgotten the word.'

'You've only got three minutes left,' Irene said.

I reached the letter V.

Paul thought for a moment. 'Valerie,' he said.

I clasped my hands in that "almost right" thing again, but they looked at me blankly. Dear god, what was wrong with them? If my slave master's whip had been real I would have used it on them. Instead, I stamped my foot and struck my forehead with the flat of my hand.

'Are you miming?' Paul asked.

The women were having hysterics. Irene had tears rolling down her cheeks; Eve and the lady from Gualchos were draped across each other on the sofa; Linda was laughing with great whoops and having difficulty remaining in her chair - although that may have had something to do with the Irish Cream.

I wheeled and faced them. 'Yes,' I said cuttingly, 'I imagine you've discovered by now that they're all easy when you've written them.' They laughed even harder.

Our hostess from Gualchos's husband had been drinking steadily, unobtrusively, all evening, slumped low in his chair. He had said nothing during my charade and seemed to be in a near-coma. I turned to him in desperation and discovered he'd disappeared below the table. Wonderful! I could see us ending up with *How Green Was My Valerie*. But, in his own quiet way, he was still participating. I heard two distinct slaps as his hands hit the edge of the table and he hauled himself up until his face appeared. He looked close to death, but he said, quite clearly, *'How Green Was My Valley'* before he slid back under the table.

CHAPTER TWENTY-TWO

The next day, the four of us crawled out of bed at noon. We were untalkative over lunch and afterwards drove to Castell in the Seat Panda that Eve and Michael had hired at Malaga airport. The sky was blue; the sun shone with July ferocity; and we spent the afternoon at the beach, recovering. While we were there we noticed a band of cloud sitting on the mountains in the north. It didn't appear to be moving, just loitering there. When we arrived back at the *cortijo* the clouds had drifted closer and Sierra de Lujar, our nearest high peak, was hidden. I didn't think that the clouds were threatening and I was unconcerned.

That night we went to bed early and I was asleep in moments. After a few hours I was woken up by rain pounding against the tiles. I lay in bed listening. The rain was heavier than I could ever remember. I got up, pulled on shorts and a tee shirt, and went downstairs to the lounge. The power was off. I opened the door. There was a sound I had never heard before - a roaring coming from the *barranco*. I stepped out of the door, down the steps, and on to the path. It wasn't there any more. My legs went from under me and water spun me sideways. The mule path was now a tributary of the *barranco*, with two feet of water hurtling past the house. I scrambled on all fours to the terrace and went inside and fetched a torch. The rain was a solid wall; water was sheeting off the roof onto the terrace; everywhere was running water, all of it channelling into the path.

I had to check that the vehicles were all right and I started to make my way down to the *barranco* via the high bank at the side of the path. The ground had turned to mud and, almost immediately, I slipped and dropped the torch. I grabbed at it, but it slid down the bank into the water. I managed to stand upright at the top of the bank, holding on to the branches of a fig tree, and waited and watched. Every few seconds, lightning revealed the scene in a split-second of brilliance before I was again in total blackness and thunder exploded a moment later. The roar of the *barranco* drowned out all other sounds. Our *campo* looked like a paddy field. A waterfall was pouring over the side of the Rubité road. Los Morales was a blur through the rain. I thought I saw Fra'quito on his balcony but I couldn't be sure. The next flash it was empty. The *barranco* was a swollen body of water racing past the bottom of what had once been our path, with the new tributary pouring into it. I needed to get closer to see the vehicles. In short stages, I progressed along the bank, testing and then holding onto handfuls of grass and weeds. If I had slipped and fallen, I feared that, like the sheep and goats of 15 years ago, I would have ended up in the sea at Castell. I reached the canes at the edge of the *barranco* and worked my way along them until I was

260

level with the vehicles. At my first sight of them I felt sick; the water in the *barranco* was a torrent that had risen to just below the side windows of the Bedford, and was battering against the back doors and erupting onto the roof. The smaller, lighter Seat was in front of the van and partly protected. The flashes of lightning were becoming less frequent; the storm was moving south towards Castell. It was like watching intermittent frames of sepia film, with lengthening periods of darkness. I saw the Seat lurch, as though someone had released its anchor, and it moved away from the Bedford. I had glimpses of it as it bobbed down the *barranco* towards the *rambla* before it disappeared round a curve.

The water was still rising; it was now above the level of the Bedford's windows and pouring in through the missing windscreen. I thought that the weight of the water would hold the van firm but, almost immediately, it shifted and moved sideways. As it slewed, the force of the water lifted the back, pushing the front down and forward. It ground along for ten yards before it came to a halt diagonally across the *barranco*, its nose buried in the mud, and was pounded by the water. I continued to watch, but it had stuck fast. Eventually, I turned away; there was nothing left to see. The rain had eased and the front path was no longer going to sweep me away, but the torrent had caused massive erosion, making craters a foot deep and exposing rocks and tree roots. I saw that there was a light up at the house. Linda was in the kitchen; she had lit a hurricane lamp.

'The van's half-buried and full of water. The Seat's

261

been washed away. The water in the *barranco* is shoulder high and it's very dangerous. I'm going to wake Mike and show him; otherwise he'll never believe it.'

I woke Michael, grabbed another torch, and we clambered down what was left of the path to the *barranco*.

He whistled. 'Bloody hell! Where's the Seat?'

'Probably half way to Castell. It was doing ten knots the last time I saw it.'

In the morning the *barranco* was back to a trickle and in a day or two it would be impossible to tell what had occurred. The van hadn't moved any further and the engine compartment and interior were full of silt. The Seat was three hundred yards away in the *rambla,* wedged in a clump of oleander bushes. The *rambla* had been rearranged and the track to Castell erased; it was now a boulder-strewn water course, still flowing strongly. I walked down to La Venta. Everyone was counting the cost. Greenhouses had been carried away, topsoil washed from fields, rooms flooded, paths and steps undermined. The *rambla* and the track to Ferrer were impassable and the Rubité road was cut. No one had electricity. I saw José and told him what had happened. He said he was sorry, but he could have said that everyone did warn me.

I walked back to the *barranco* and poked around the van. It would be easy enough to dig out, but I didn't really believe it would go again. I felt depressed and wandered up the *barranco* to the deposit to check our water supply. It was full of brown, silty water and a thirty-yard stretch of the channel that José and I had worked on had been swept away. It was not too bad - a morning's work. I decided to go back to the house for a mattock to repair the channel. I was putting off cleaning up the Bedford and assessing the damage. I was not ready to face the prospect of living here without it.

On the way up to the house I took a detour. I wanted to check on a nightingales' nest close by. We had listened to their virtuoso performances day and night for weeks without seeing them and we had begun to suspect that they were invisible, until one day I spotted a flash of chestnut as one darted into a clump of brambles on the bank beneath the channel. Afterwards, we sat with our binoculars trained on the brambles watching these inconspicuous, shy birds dash in and out, feeding their young. As I came closer, I saw that the brambles were festooned with twigs and a tangle of leaves and grass. I was immediately fearful; I parted the stems and peered inside. The nest had gone. I searched around and found it mangled at the bottom of the bank. There was no sign of the adult birds, but lying on the ground nearby were three young nightingales, their feathers matted and mud-streaked. Above the clump of brambles, the earth wall of the channel had given way and water had cascaded over the nest, tearing it apart. I was devastated - I had felt certain they would survive. At that moment, the death of the young nightingales affected me more than the damage to the Bedford.

I made my way up to the house. The front path needed major rebuilding. I was trying to decide if that was more important than repairing the channel when it occurred to me that I ought to check the shed and make sure that the Ossa hadn't been carried away by a torrent of water. The way things were going, I was pessimistic about what I would find, but the Ossa was safe and dry and had a smug look about it. Well, at least that was something. When I arrived on the terrace, Linda was hanging out sodden mats and Michael was clearing up branches from around the house. Eve was inside, checking the hire-car documents, making sure they had ticked the right insurance boxes. They had all been down to the *barranco* to look at the van.

Linda looked miserable and I gave her a hug. 'Come on, it could be worse,' I said. 'At least the Ossa's okay and I've found the Seat. It didn't end up in Castell; it's a few hundred yards away in the *rambla*. It needs pulling out of some bushes but, you never know, it might start first time.'

It didn't. We hauled it out of the oleander bushes, picked the debris out of the engine compartment, and Michael sat in and turned the key. Nothing happened, other than water squelched out of the seat and saturated his trousers. We left the Seat to dry out, with the bonnet and doors open, and went back to the house. I spent the morning repairing the channel and did enough work on the front path to enable us to use it without breaking our legs. Lastly, I went across to the brambles and dug a small hole at the bottom of the bank and buried the three nightingales. After lunch, Michael and I went back to the Seat. Taking it in turns to push, we eventually started it, but it was impossible to drive. The engine alternately roared like a tractor or faded and cut out. The car progressed in great lunges, hurtling forward for perhaps fifty yards before it died and had to be push-started again.

'You can't drive this anywhere,' I said. 'We'll have to go into Castell and ring the hire company. We'll tell them what's happened and ask them for another car.'

Linda and I went into Castell on the Ossa. It rose to the occasion, relishing its elevated status to *numero uno* and handled the reorganised *rambla* with authority. The deluge of water from the night before had nearly gone. It was still flowing in a narrow stream past La Venta and the turn to Ferrer, but after that there were only occasional pools. Paths and tracks that had led to people's homes were obliterated and all the way to Castell we saw men and women working with mattocks repairing the damage. On several of the wider sections, the water had deposited a smooth layer of silt. It was like riding into snow. The Ossa sank in; I opened the throttle and it powered through, sending an arc of grey mud behind us. Close to the mouth of the *rambla,* we passed the cemetery. It was peaceful, undisturbed by the previous night's devastation, its inhabitants safely tucked up inside their vaults in the white walls. The municipal rubbish tip, which had sprawled down the bank of the *rambla* alongside the cemetery, had vanished. I had always thought it odd that they were situated so close together. I had seen pigs' intestines and whole carcasses of mules dumped there, and truck-loads of rotting melons. The smell was horrendous, but I don't suppose the residents of the cemetery minded. I stopped the bike at the top of the hill leading into Castell. The view was astonishing. For a mile out to sea, from the point where the *rambla* runs into the

Mediterranean, there was a channel, three hundred yards wide, of brown water. From there, it spread out either side, like a massive hammerhead, as far as we could see. The rubbish from the *rambla,* which had collected there since the last big *tormenta,* had been washed into the Mediterranean. There was debris floating close to the shore: logs, pallets, metal drums, tangled rafts of plastic sheeting and branches - and, no doubt, a few burnt-out wooden tables.

We rode down to the plaza and Linda rang the hire company while I changed the spark plug - I wasn't taking any chances on the journey back up the *rambla.* I was cleaning my hands on a rag when she came back.

'They don't believe me. They think it's feminine whimsy. They said it is not possible that their car has been washed away. You'll have to talk to them.'

I strode over to the telephone booth. 'Listen,' I said, 'simply because you are sitting in a dry office in Malaga, it doesn't mean that the rest of Spain is. Last night in the *sierras* there was a *tormenta,* and the *camino* where the Seat was parked became a *rio* and your car turned into a boat and went floating off. The car filled up with water; it doesn't go and it needs major repairs. We want another car and we want it this afternoon.' I told them that we would get the car to Castell plaza and they said they would send a driver with another car to meet us there at 6pm.

'Simple,' I said to Linda, smiling. 'It's just a question of being positive. I'll leave you to handle motorbike cops and I'll deal with hire-car people - and you might have noticed that I don't need to wear a short skirt.'

I was starting to feel better.

Michael and I had an erratic and exhilarating drive to Castell in the Seat. Several 4X4 vehicles had already been up and down the *rambla* and had made a rough track down the centre. In the absence of any better option, we followed it. Sections were alternately rocky and cratered or soft and boggy. They were awful driving conditions, but there is absolutely nothing like a hire car to bring out the rally driver in a person. For the periods we weren't digging it out or pushing it, the Seat tore along at breakneck speed with either Mike or I at the wheel while the other ran along behind. It took us two hours to travel the five miles into Castell. In the plaza we exchanged keys with an earnest young man sent by the hire company and Michael signed another piece of paper. We left the young man walking round the car shaking his head while we went into *El Terrible* for a beer. When we came out, the Seat and the young man had gone. I imagine he had an eventful trip back to Malaga.

Michael drove the replacement Seat at walking pace up the *rambla*, picking his way around the obstacles - he felt sure that if he damaged another one of their cars they'd put him on a world-wide blacklist - and several times I got out to roll boulders out of our path and help push the car through the boggy sections. When we arrived at Los Sanchez the power had been restored, there was little evidence that there had ever been a storm, and Linda and Eve were in the kitchen, producing wonderful smells.

Eve and Michael had only a few days of their holiday

left and the next day they went off exploring in their new hire car. Linda and I dug out the van, shovelled out the silt from inside, hosed down the engine compartment, and left it to dry. I took the battery up to the house and put it on charge, and in the afternoon we went down to see if it would start. I turned the key and the gauges on the dashboard worked. I pushed the ignition button and there was a dull clunk. The starter motor had seized, but the Bedford had its secret weapon - a starting handle. I cranked the engine and it started on the third turn - but it wasn't right. The engine was misfiring; it sounded bronchial and there was a rattle of phlegm deep inside. But the fact that it went at all showed the toughness of the Bedford. I put it in reverse and spluttered back up the *barranco* to the bottom of the path. I would take all the pieces apart that I was capable of taking apart, wash, clean and grease everything, put it all back together again and trust in the gods. On the way up to the house, I showed Linda the nightingales' nest. It was so sad, so ... *unnecessary.*

A week later, a giant grader, which had been commandeered from nearby road works, crawled up the *rambla,* bulldozing a road all the way to La Venta. For a few days, the surface was as smooth as the M5, until a tractor with caterpillar tracks turned it into corrugated iron.

The van was never the same. Twice, I dismantled and cleaned the starter motor; I fiddled with the electric wiring and replaced fuses, but I could not get the van to start on the ignition. After a few days, the connecting pins on the starting handle sheared and, from then on, we had to park it on a slope. To do our shopping, we free-wheeled most of the way to Castell, left it on the hill leading in, and walked the rest. It limped back up the *rambla*, firing on three cylinders, coughing, backfiring, and puffing steam from the radiator. I asked Paul to come over and take a look at it. He rolled around underneath the Bedford with a torch, and then performed some clever mechanic's tricks, such as looking for droplets of water on the end of the dipstick, checking for bubbles of exhaust gas in the radiator, and sticking a piece of wood between the side of the engine and his ear, like a stethoscope.

He finished his inspection and shook his head. 'If I had all the tools and a hoist or a pit - which I haven't - and if I could get all the parts - which I can't - then I could repair it. But even then it wouldn't be worth it.'

I thanked Paul. It was what I had expected. It was slowly dying.

CHAPTER TWENTY-THREE

Summer drifted on. Each day, by 10 o'clock, it was too hot to do anything except swim in the sea. The rubbish from the *rambla* washed up on the beach at Castell and formed into a ridge of branches, canes, and splintered lengths of timber, of metal drums and rusty tin cans, and thousands of shoes and bottles, the whole lot entwined in great swathes of plastic sheeting from the greenhouses - a three-feet high ribbon curling along the beach at the high-water line. Municipal workers filled trucks with it and dumped it at the tip - where it lay waiting to be washed back out to sea in the next *tormenta*. It didn't matter how many times they cleared it from the beach, more arrived on the next tide. The holidaymakers pretended it wasn't there and sunbathed around it.

The Bedford was in decline. We now had to fill the radiator two or three times on the way back from Castell and, unless we had a load to carry, we used the Ossa, which was behaving but it didn't like the heat. On our trips along the coast to Motril and Adra, the engine almost glowed and the fibreglass panel alongside became scorched brown. The Ossa was happier on the rough tracks in the mountains; it was not designed for the road. The suspension was too spongy and the knobbly tyres were wrong for the fast stretches of tarmac. It bucked and skittered round the curves and bounced along the straights, with the vibration loosening our teeth. But we forgave it every one of its faults. Without it, we would have been marooned.

August passed slowly. Our summer guests had left and no more would arrive until next year. We still occasionally drove the Bedford, but each time we did something new went wrong. One by one, the horn, the headlights and the brake lights failed, and finally the indicators - which made turning left lethal. The hand brake no longer worked and, when we parked it on the hill at Castell, we left it in gear and put bricks under the wheels - but we always feared that someone would come along and take them for their building works. One day, on the way back from Castell, a frenzied hammering came from the engine, and the Bedford coughed once apologetically and died. I asked Paul to look at it again and he told me that no amount of work - short of replacing the engine, the radiator, the electrical system, and just about everything else - would make the van go. We now had the Ossa as our only means of transport.

We had been at Los Sanchez for two years and the sense of aimlessness that we had felt at the beginning of summer increased. We had been able to justify our hedonistic lifestyle during the heat of July and August, but now that the weather was cooler we had to do something. We had discovered that a life of partial self-sufficiency alone did not hold enough challenges for us and, for the first time, we were without a clear purpose. We needed a project to stimulate us and we needed to earn money. Our financial position was far less healthy than when we arrived. We had spent more than we had budgeted renovating the house, and the cost of living over the last two years had risen dramatically, with the result that we could no longer live on the interest from our savings and we were drawing on our capital. We needed to buy another van or a car, but it was almost impossible to find a cheap second hand vehicle locally. Here, the people bought their vehicles new and kept them until either they or their vehicles died.

Legally, we could not work, although no one was likely to object if we grew a marketable crop on our land, as José had done, but the return was small. It was only when you had a greenhouse that you made a good living - you produced three crops a year, including the earliest crop of runner beans in Europe, when the price was at its highest - but in the open *campo* you grew two crops and your beans became ripe at the same time as everyone else's, when the prices were sometimes so low it was hardly worth the effort of picking them.

During the time we had been here, our way of life had been superficially little different from the locals - although, of course, there was one very large difference. We were only playing at their lifestyle. We had the freedom of choice that they did not. We were happy pretending to be Spanish peasants - knowing that, at any time we wanted to, we could pack our bags and go back to the lives we had left – but we were not prepared to live here with our capital diminishing and subsistence farming as our only option. It had been a wonderful, extraordinary adventure and it had enriched us more than we had ever imagined, but we knew that we could not stay - too many factors had converged which gave us no choice. Now, we were marking time, waiting for something to happen which would provide us with the impetus to leave. Neither of us knew it then, but it already had.

The last time I drove the Bedford was when Paul towed me to the customs office at the port of Motril. I handed the log book and the keys to the official and told him I was forced to abandon the van in Spain because it would not make the journey back to England. He asked me to repeat what I had said and, when there was no possibility of a misunderstanding, he looked devastated; I had just presented him with two week's paperwork.

Linda had spent the morning in Motril while Paul and I dealt with the customs, and after Paul had dropped us back at Los Sanchez and gone home, Linda said, 'I am *embarazada.*' She was smiling.

'What are you embarrassed about?'

'It doesn't mean that.'

'What does it mean?'

'It means we're leaving.'

She had placed the open dictionary on the kitchen table. The handle of a teaspoon pointed to the word.

'That is truly wonderful.' I kissed her. 'When is it due?'

'In March. We've lots of time.'

We had decided that if Linda became pregnant we would go back to England or Australia. There were too

273

many things against having a baby here, one of the main ones being the distance to the nearest hospital. Up until recently, before people started to own cars, the local babies were delivered by the shepherds and, in cases of emergency, they still were. The prospect of Little Onion, either drunk or sober, delivering our first child was motivation enough to leave.

We had now made the decision to leave, but I was equally determined that we would come back, and that when we did we would be better prepared. I felt that we couldn't just lock up the house and walk away – we needed to make a tangible commitment to return – or else we would slip, without really noticing it, into the routine of married life with young children, a hefty mortgage and me tightly encased in my loss adjuster's suit, with the years stretching out in front of me – all the things that had made me want to escape in the first place. We needed a project to come back to and I knew exactly what it would be, but it meant spending more of our dwindling capital.

On the hillside above Los Sanchez were the crumbling remains of a tiny, two-roomed house. Its roof had collapsed and only one stone wall was sound. It perched precariously on a steep slope and was in danger of slipping away entirely. The surrounding half acre of hillside with its scattering of almond trees, as well as a flat field with half a day's water rights from the *barranco,* were on the same title as the ruined house. Both the section of hillside and the flat field adjoined our land. The property was owned by José and Anna, a couple in their late seventies, who lived in a village half-

274

way to Motril, and who had not worked the land for years, although they still came with their family each August to pick the almonds. To rebuild and extend the ruin was the perfect project and, with the increasing number of foreigners moving into the area, I felt sure that it would be a good investment. I estimated that it would take me at least eighteen months to carry out the work and while I was doing it we could look for other employment. We could act as consultants to foreigners buying properties in the area – we were now experts at unravelling the tangle of bureaucracy that blighted these purchases, or perhaps there would be a demand for a part-time, English-speaking loss adjuster in Motril. Of course, obtaining work visas would be a nightmare, but Spain was making noises about entering the Common Market and the laws on allowing foreigners to work here were bound to become less strict. I spoke about it to Linda.

'All right,' she said, 'providing we can buy it at a fair price. You know how much people are now asking for these ruins. Oh, and also, when we come back, we are not going to be living on the poverty line.'

'Absolutely,' I said. 'Anything you say, darling.'

I now needed to work out the best way to approach José and Anna. It would have to done obliquely. For us to simply ride over to their house and state that we were interested in buying their property would be fatal – they would ask at least three times what it was worth. I went to see Francisco *Alcalde*.

'José is a *comunista*.' Francisco still judged people by which side they had fought on in the civil war. He thought about the matter for a few moments and then tapped the side of his nose in a conspiratorial fashion. 'The person to see is Miguel de Plato.' He whispered the words as though he was revealing something that the secret police would like to have known.

Miguel de Plato was a local *albanil,* He was a large, imposing man who made a good living working mainly on foreigners' houses. He had additionally gained a reputation as a useful person to have sitting in on the negotiations by foreigners to purchase a property, although I had never fully understood his role in these transactions. He spoke no language other than Spanish, yet he somehow managed to act as a mediator between the parties. Someone who had used his services told me that his very presence seemed to have a calming effect on the proceedings and controlled any excesses by either party. It was only if the negotiations went off the rails that he would intervene and become the independent voice of reason. I visited Miguel at his home and explained that we were possibly interested in buying José and Anna's property and we wanted him to make a subtle approach on our behalf. His task was to portray us as far-from-certain, prospective purchasers. Miguel said that he would be prepared to act in this matter and that, regardless of whether the sale went through, he charged a flat fee, which was the equivalent of what he would charge for five day's work as an *albanil.* The price was huge, but if we were successful then the money would have been well spent. Despite Francisco *Alcalde's* suggestive nose tapping, Miguel's highly-developed capitalistic approach to life made me seriously doubt that he was even remotely connected to the communist party.

The next day Miguel called on José and Anna and told them that the *extranjeros* at Los Sanchez were thinking about buying more land next to their own, which meant either Fraquito and Adela's field, a section of hillside owned by a couple in Cordoba, or José and Anna's property. If they were interested in selling they would have to move quickly because soon we would be returning to England and the chance might be lost forever. Miguel pointed out that there would not be many people who would want to buy a flat field that became a lake every time the *barranco* flooded, and a steep piece of hillside that was accessed only by a mule path. To them, the tiny ruin sliding down the side of the hill had no value, but to me it did. I knew that because it was an existing dwelling I could rebuild it without having to go through the virtually impossible task of obtaining planning permission from the local mayor.

Miguel de Plato came to see us in the afternoon. 'They didn't say so, but I feel that they want to sell. We will go and see them tomorrow morning at their home.'

Miguel drove us to José and Anna's house and they showed us into their dim formal lounge which was reserved for such occasions. The room was suitably dreary and it smelled of mothballs and lavender air freshener. For twenty minutes we talked of anything but the reason why we were all there until at last Miguel de Plato looked at his watch, sighed heavily and murmured a ponderous, '*Bueno.*'

José had been waiting for the cue and announced without preamble, 'The land is fertile and it has water rights.'

I blinked. 'Yes, but only half a day out of ten.'

'That is still a lot of water.'

'Not when the *barranco* is becoming less each year.'

'I could sell the land tomorrow to foreigners.'

'Possibly you could.'

'They would build a house in the field. You would not like neighbours right next to you.'

'They would never get permission to build. It is classified for rural use only and, anyway, when the *barranco* floods, the field goes under water.'

'You have just told me that the water in the *barranco* is less nowadays.'

'That is so, but it only needs one *tormenta* to make it flood. *We* know all about that.' I saw Miguel smother a grin.

'We are not desperate to sell.'

I smiled. 'That is good, because we are not desperate to buy.'

The negotiations lurched to and fro, with José extolling the qualities of the property while I countered with the negatives. Anna chimed in to support her husband and Linda and Miguel watched and listened in silence. Suddenly it was half-time. Anna went in to the kitchen and returned with a tray of cold drinks and biscuits. Miguel must have told them that Linda was pregnant because Anna started to fuss around her, handed her a cushion for the small of her back and started to talk about her own child-bearing days. José changed tactics and, in the pauses between Anna's reminiscences, he told us how the land had been in his family for generations; it was part of his heritage; he could barely bring himself to part with it. Finally, he mentioned the price for which he might possibly be persuaded to sell - which was more than twice what we were prepared to pay.

I thanked them for their time and their hospitality, told them that we were not rich tourists and Linda and I got up to leave. Miguel said something to José that I did not understand and gestured with his hand for us to sit down. He then spoke very rapidly to José and Anna. From what Linda and I could make out, he told them that we had lived in the region long enough to know the correct value of the land and we would not pay a crazy price like a foreigner who had come straight from Malaga airport. We were shortly going back to England and there was no guarantee when we would return. If José and Anna wanted to sell, then now was the time to do it. We sat down again and José and I continued to negotiate. The price crept lower until it was within ten per cent of our figure and José stated that he would not go a peseta lower. He was not giving the land to us as a present. He was becoming agitated and I was wavering and thinking that ten per cent was really not that much more than our maximum when, with deft timing, Miguel seized the moment. He cleared his throat noisily and glanced at Linda and then at me. He tilted his head to one side and raised his eyebrows. The room remained frozen like that for a few seconds while I gazed at Linda until, at last, she nodded.

'*Vale,*' I said and repeated the price. 'Okay, we agree.'

Everyone shook everyone else's hand and we straightaway filled out and signed the contract, with Miguel and a neighbour witnessing the signatures. We had made our commitment to return.

During our last week, after Linda had gone up to bed, I walked around the house, going from room to room to look at the work we had done, gazing at objects as though it was the first time I had seen them - at our furniture that we had such fun collecting, and had stripped down, repaired and reupholstered - and I thought of the traumas and difficulties we had bringing it here. I went into the bathroom and laughed. When we come back I'll rip it all out and start again. I looked at the antique lock on the inside of the kitchen door. It had always fascinated me; it was the largest lock I have ever seen; the metal box that housed the mechanism was the size of a handbag, and carrying the key around was like having a trowel in your pocket – but, despite its massive size, it was still a basic two-lever mortice lock that a schoolboy could open with a penknife. I went into the lounge last and looked at the heavy red floor tiles from Motril that had tested our patience and our backs, and remembered the day when, in frustration, I hurled a tile across the room and broke it against the far wall; and I would slide my foot across the floor to feel the ridge where we were never able to make them level. Before I went upstairs to Linda, I turned off the lights and stood in the darkness and felt the character of the house. I breathed deeply. The house no longer smelt of must and tallow; it had absorbed the smells of our cooking, of coffee ground every morning, and of bunches of dried herbs and wood smoke, and lavender polish and teak oil, and joss sticks and Linda's perfumes - it smelt of us.

I didn't want to leave here; I would miss this house that we had invested so much in; I loved this beautiful valley; this raw, powerful, unforgiving country with its fierce climate; and I loved the people and their warmth and their openness and their generosity. I didn't want to forget it; I didn't want to forget the tiniest part of it. I didn't want it ever to leave me.

The day before we left, I went to see Emilio at the *moto* repairers in the back streets of Castell. The Ossa and Emilio were good friends and I was Emilio's best customer. His workshop was crammed with *motos* in various stages of dismemberment and he was peering into the gearbox of an ancient machine. His blue overalls were solid with oil. You could have wrung them out and filled the sump of the Bedford.

'Ah, it's you – *hola*! What's happened this time?'

'Nothing. We're going back to England and while we're away I want you to fix the Ossa properly so that it starts every time, doesn't cover us both in oil, and stops cutting out for no good reason.'

Emilio looked suddenly happy. This was work he dreamed of - work that he could do during his slack periods, with no pressure on him to complete, and for which he could charge pretty much what he liked.

'You can depend on me,' he said. 'I believe I know what is needed. To start off with, a new ignition box and carburettor, and replacement seals on the suspension and exhaust.' He paused before continuing with the list of things that needed to be done. It was very long and, as he became more technical, he began to lose me. I started to worry and, when he mentioned

281

something about rebuilding the engine and gearbox, it sounded as though it would be cheaper to buy a brand new bike when we came back. I realised that I might as well give Emilio my cheque book and I hastily interrupted him.

'I'll write and let you know our address and you can send me a written quote of what needs doing together with the cost, and then I can decide what I want done.'

I left the Ossa with him and Paul gave me a lift back to the house.

The last evening, we tried to finish off the opened bottles of wine and spirits in the kitchen cupboard. It was an ambitious plan and late at night, after Linda had given up and gone upstairs, I stumbled around the house, utterly miserable and maudlin. I turned off the light in the lounge, made my way to the centre of the room, and promptly fell over a chair I couldn't remember being there. Linda came back down and switched on the light.

'I can't bear to go, Linda. I want to die here. I want a corner of our field to be forever England.'

'Come on, up you get. You'll feel better in the morning.'

The following day, a steady stream of neighbours visited us to say goodbye. So many people had come to the house over the past week to wish us well, some of whom we hardly knew. We hadn't realised it before, but we had brought new life to the valley and they didn't want to see us go. It was wonderful and heart warming and we kept repeating that we would come back; that this was only temporary and we would see them all again. It was hard saying goodbye to José - he had shepherded us through those early months and become such a part of our lives. It was the perfect situation for José to deliver one of his flowery speeches that he enjoyed so much and, by the end of it, we were all in tears.

Antonio the *mulero* was the last to visit us, just before Paul was due to take us to the bus stop in Castell. The early antagonism over the straw episode was long forgotten and we were now friends. He tied his mule to a post on the terrace and stuck his unshaven face around the kitchen door. He was grinning and his breath smelt of wine.

'When you have your baby in England, it is very important you use this.' He handed us one of those medical tags that nurses put round the ankles of new-born babies so that they don't mix them up. He had written on it:

FABRICA EN ESPAÑA

(MADE IN SPAIN)

10685306R00167

Printed in Great Britain
by Amazon.co.uk, Ltd.,
Marston Gate.